PLAYS BY DONALD FREED

357 W 20th St., NY NY 10011
212 627-1055

PLAYS BY DONALD FREED
Copyright © 1990 by Donald Freed

All rights reserved. This work is fully protected under the copyright laws of the United States of America. No part of this publication may be photocopied, reproduced, stored in a retrieval system, or transmitted, in any form or by any means, electronic, mechanical, recording, or otherwise, without the prior permission of the publisher. Additional copies of this play are available from the publisher.

Written permission is required for live performance of any sort. This includes readings, cuttings, scenes, and excerpts. For amateur and stock performances, please contact Broadway Play Publishing Inc. For all other rights contact: Stephen Lisk, ICM, 8899 Beverly Blvd, LA CA 90048, 213 550-4255.

First printing: September 1990
ISBN: 0-88145-088-X

Book design: Marie Donovan
Word processing: WordMarc Composer Plus
Typographic controls: Xerox Ventura Publisher, Professional Extension
Typeface: Palatino
Printed on acid-free paper and bound in the USA.

CONTENTS

About the Author .... *v*
Meet Donald Freed, by Richard Stayton .... *vii*
ALFRED AND VICTORIA: A LIFE 1
CHILD OF LUCK 33
IS HE STILL DEAD? 87

ABOUT THE AUTHOR

Donald Freed's plays include INQUEST (directed by Alan Schneider), SECRET HONOR (directed by Robert Altman), CIRCE & BRAVO (with Faye Dunaway, directed by Harold Pinter), THE QUARTERED MAN, VETERAN'S DAY (with Jack Lemmon and Michael Gambon), and THE WHITE CROW.

His awards include the Rockefeller Award, Louis B Mayer Award, Unicorn Prize, Gold Medal Award, Berlin Critics Award, and the NEA award for "Distinguished Writing".

His books and films include AGONY IN NEW HAVEN, EXECUTIVE ACTION (novel and film with Mark Lane), THE GLASSHOUSE TAPES, THE SPYMASTER, IN SEARCH OF COMMON GROUND (with Erik Erikson, Kai Erikson, Huey P Newton), THE EXISTENTIALISM OF ALBERTO MORAROA (with Joan Ross), and DEATH IN WASHINGTON.

His upcoming plays and films include SOLIDARITY!, LOVE AND SHADOWS (from the novel by Isabel Allende), and SOCRATES MUST DIE (with Edward Asner).

MEET DONALD FREED
by Richard Stayton

"Donald Freed is a writer of blazing imagination, courage and insight. His work is a unique and fearless marriage of politics and art. I take my hat off to him."
—Harold Pinter

Late in 1989 Donald Freed was recuperating in his West Los Angeles home from brutal assaults when the phone rang. Should he answer? Or let the machine record a message while he rested? His wounds were the worst a playwright can experience: creative castration by drama critics.

What had been Freed's sin?

While touring England's northern industrial cities, where unemployment compels political debate, Freed's anti-war VETERAN'S DAY had been greeted by critical acclaim. But when the play reached London, "impassioned political dynamite" mutated into "hysterical rantings." London reviewers didn't review VETERAN'S DAY—they gang-raped it.

Now, feeling like My Lai, Freed needed rest and recuperation. Let the phone ring, to hell with the literary wars! But this was a Sunday and.... He answered to hear a familiar baritone on the London end of the telephone line.

"Are you sitting down?" Harold Pinter asked Freed. "Hold on to your chair while I read a column published in *The Times*."

Britain's greatest living playwright proceeded to read from that Sunday's London *Times* opinion page: "...The assault of the critics which drove this work out after two months loses us a piece of distinguished, moving and morally eloquent writing.... The denunciation of conventional war, with its conventional mutilations and dementia, and the hatred expressed for the cardboard great ones of government, was too fine for the play's good.... We have lost the taste for eloquence. It is shocking to let such writing die in front of thinned-down last-week audiences. In a tense, fierce way VETERAN'S DAY addresses the reality of which humankind cannot bear very much."

Neither Freed nor Pinter knew the journalist. Clearly, Edward Pearce's column was inspired solely by the play. Such praise from a stranger resurrected Freed's commitment while supporting Pinter's belief in Freed's talent. After all, Pinter had hoped to act in VETERAN'S DAY, until writing responsibilities interfered, then encouraged Michael Gambon to take his place onstage opposite Jack Lemmon. And, as columnist Pearce noted: "Both men [Gambon and Lemmon] are too discerning to pick a duff play."

"That shall go on my tombstone," Freed said months later of the appropriately titled *Last Word* column. "The play has closed, so the piece was pure, free, and gratuitous. It was an essay on culture, eloquence and on the artist's relationship to the audience. Would I trade that glorious epitaph for mundane money reviews? I would have at previous times in my life, but not any more. Now I do not demand of the theater that it supports me. You can't make a living as a playwright, not in America."

Freed, the third most prolific playwright in Los Angeles (after Neil Simon and John Steppling) with *seventeen* produced plays, not make a living from the stage? Ever since attending the Art Institute of Chicago's Goodman Theater program in the early 1950s. Freed has been a man of, in, and for the theater. His INQUEST: THE U.S. VS. JULIUS AND ETHEL ROSENBERG enjoyed a respectable Broadway run in 1970. Robert Altman adapted Freed's hit play SECRET HONOR: THE LAST TESTAMENT OF RICHARD M NIXON" (1983, co-written with attorney Arnold M. Stone) into an award-winning film. After seeing Altman's version, Pinter phoned Freed to express his admiration — "The thrill of a lifetime," remembers Freed. Soon Pinter was directing Freed's CIRCE & BRAVO (1985) in London, with Faye Dunaway portraying a justifiably paranoid First Lady.

Not make a living after all this? But the economic explanation is blunt and grim: Freed's work exists on the far, far side of Neil Simon. Freed unapologetically embraces the unthinkable and unpardonable: politics. Worse, his writing agenda isn't hidden, his mission never covert. When he speaks of "The Dream Factory," he doesn't mean Hollywood — he's speaking of Washington, D.C.

"Politics are our flesh and blood," Freed insists. "A writer lives in the middle of politics. There's no such thing as non-political. You may want to put a spin on it. You can try to deny it, but that's a political decision. And you deny it out of fear. Then you have what happened in the 1940s and 1950s in this country. Basically, America has never recovered from the McCarthy era. We are not free, said Artaud, and the sky can still fall on our heads, and the theater is created to teach us that first of all."

Other play titles more clearly define Freed's agenda. THE WHITE CROW: EICHMANN IN JERUSALEM (1984) explores the Holocaust from a psychosexual perspective. ALFRED AND VICTORIA: A LIFE (1986), although sounding like nostalgia for the Victorian royal couple, is actually a love story between millionaire Alfred Bloomingdale and his doomed mistress Vicky Morgan. THE QUARTERED MAN (1985) is what might result from a Dostoevsky and Graham Greene collaboration: an "Our Man in Nicaragua" with the brothers Raskolnokov portraying a CIA agent.

More overtly political is Freed's literary output: detective novels such as THE SPYMASTER, THE CHINA CARD, and EXECUTIVE ACTION; histories like THE KILLING OF RFK and THE SECRET LIFE OF RONALD REAGAN.

Freed is clearly no escapist. Not only does he pay the price at the box office, he finds that America's blacklist is still operative. Something more than money drives our playwrights into writing tame "entertainment," says Freed: Political Censorship.

"Serious writing in this country has the secret police in it, up to their ear," Freed says. Paranoia? Freed speaks from experience.

Thanks to the Freedom of Information Act, Freed owns documents proving what happens to writers who dare to explore politics. According to a U.S. Government memorandum, FBI Associate Director William Sullivan, at the insistence of Judge Irving Kaufman (who earlier sentenced the Rosenbergs to the electric chair), instructed an FBI agent to investigate INQUEST.

Dated May 2, 1969, the memorandum states: "Judge Kaufman was alarmed that *The New York Times* reviewed this play two weeks in a row...which was highly unusual. Judge Kaufman indicated that he understands the play is critical of the Director, the prosecutor, and Judge Kaufman who was the trial judge in the Rosenberg case. The Judge added that he felt the Attorney General should be informed, and the Director advised that he would let the Attorney General know."

And then the agent writing the memorandum, "Mr. W. A. Branigan," poses as theater critic: "(The play) is propaganda rather than drama. The author is Donald Martin Freed." Finally, he concludes with: "No identifiable derogatory information on (the play's director) or any of the actors or actresses in Cleveland, New York or Bureau files."

Freed's file on the government's surveillance of INQUEST also contains a letter of gratitude from Judge Kaufman thanking FBI Director J. Edgar Hoover for "the background information of the gentleman responsible for writing the play." Another FBI memo to Associate Director Sullivan reports the receipt of Freed's script and outlines its plot, ending with a chilling "RECOMMENDATION: This matter will be followed closely."

It was. Freed's INQUEST file contains other memos, letters and documents. Letters were planted in *The New York Times* denouncing the play's allegations that the Rosenbergs were convicted out of hysteria. When the play finally opened in New York *The Times'* critic Clive Barnes' review "was cut for the first time in his career. A paragraph was removed from his review that said they should re-open the Rosenberg case."

While INQUEST was heading for Broadway, Freed was politically active with an organization titled "Friends of the Black Panther Party." This, too, did not go unnoticed. While Freed attended a conference in Oakland, California, with the Black Panthers, a mimeo flyer was circulated (a copy of which follows this introduction). "DON FREED IS A PIG," announced the leaflet. A crude drawing of a sow in police uniform leaned next to the headline: "...He is a PIG," a lousy informant who deals with his fellow PIGS, and betrays us all." The writer signed-off with "All Power to the People." The writer was an FBI operative.

In a memo from the Los Angeles FBI office to Director Hoover, dated July 9, 1969 ("Subject: Disruption of the New Left"), the strategy was outlined: "It is the desire of the Los Angeles office to neutralize FREED by the distribution of a throwaway accusing FREED of being an informant."

When Freed's film, EXECUTIVE ACTION (co-written with Mark Lane), suggested alternatives to the Warren Commission's findings on President John F. Kennedy's assassination, the C.I.A. instructed its "agents of influence worldwide" to begin a campaign to destroy Freed's reputation.

Then there are court records of the $200,000,000 (sic) suit filed by C.I.A. operative David Atlee Phillips against Freed's book on Chilean diplomat Orlando Letelier's 1976 assassination, DEATH IN WASHINGTON (co-written by political scientist Fred Landis). While revealing how the C.I.A. instigated the overthrow of the democratically elected government of Chile, a number of spies were named. And so, a group of "retired spies" founded by Phillips, the Association of Former Intelligence Officers, raised a war chest to finance the suit against Freed. More ominously, Phillips, backed by the C.I.A., found a federal judge who ruled that "national security" issues required that Phillips *not* answer questions about his espionage career. The burden fell on Freed to prove the allegations without access to evidence.

"The decision in the Phillips case has given civil liberties experts the chills," wrote Jack Anderson in his *Washington Post* column (June 12, 1983). "They point out that [U.S. District Judge Thomas Jackson's] decision, if allowed to stand, would effectively muzzle anyone who writes something the C.I.A. or its former agents don't like. The threat of a libel suit, in which the defense is shackled, is enough to scare off all but the most reckless writers and publishers."

Ex-attorney general Ramsey Clark rallied to Freed's defense: "The attempt to silence critical voices like that of Donald Freed's is very serious. They are not playing games.... This is the way it starts—think of Germany, think of Chile...."

The suit was finally settled for $1, but only after "great emotional and financial cost." A lawsuit, Freed discovered the hard way, "is a new form of censorship practiced widely during the Reagan years."

Yet Freed pushes on, despite the odds. His wife Patty, a psychology professor, says, "Nothing stops Donald. He has amazing resilience."

"Pessimism, like optimism, is simply a mood," Freed believes. "Both moods are irrelevant and childish. One must be like the ancient Greeks, beyond hope but beyond fear. As Bertrand Russell said, 'Anyone born after World War One can never know what happiness is.' Thus the lust for happy endings in our popular culture."

Odd that this most intellectual of speakers and writers is "essentially a college dropout." Always the iconoclast, Freed attended numerous universities without ever sticking to a single curriculum long enough to achieve a degree. Yet, he's taught all across the country, from Yale to Cal-Arts, focussing on Dostoevsky, Freud, mythology, linguistics, and — above all — politics.

Freed's not a zealot waving pamphlets, however. His concept of theater is rooted in the classic Athenian theater. We forget how Sophocles and Euripides were condemning through myth the disastrous Pelloponesian Wars. The earliest play we have in the Western World, Aeschylus' THE PERSIANS, is a political play. "My own idea of theater is ultra-conservative in that it tallies with the aesthetics of the Greek theater," he declares. "How can a writer ignore collossal events like the Rosenberg show-trial, the Kennedy and King assassinations, Vietnam, Watergate, Iran-Contra?"

Freed detailed his playwriting aesthetic in an introduction to the published version of INQUEST: "Here is the vocabulary of the myth of the twentieth century: film, tape, trials, technology, confessions — in short, the state and its visible paraphernalia. The infrastrucure of the myth is the agony and confrontation between Science and Magic.... The anti-myth to the magic of the State is Theatre of Fact. The anti-myth to the science of the State is Theatre of Cruelty."

This anthology offers three examples of Freed's theatrical attempts to merge Artaud and docudrama, particularly in CHILD OF LUCK. Here tragic "Oedipus Tyrannus" meets the cursed Kennedy family. The plague that devastated fifth century B.C. Athens is echoed in the year 2000 A.D. by the AIDS scourge. Within the context of backroom political convention maneuvers, Freed presents a symbolic duel of opposites: the proud Oedipus and the arrogant Kennedy clan. He molds the ancient and modern tragic hero into a futuristic Janus. In effect, Freed does what Sophocles and Shakespeare did: "Rewriting a received myth and body of communal stories."

"The two new theatres of fact and cruelty," Freed continued in his introduction, "provide a grammer, at last, for a popular drama of the twentieth century. All exponential numbers, facts and figures, names and dates and places are necessary to even begin to come close to the phenomena of our time: the death camps, the great purge trials, the Triple Revolution, and most of all the atom bomb. But for the interpretation of all these facts it also requires cruelty. The spectator must be given a choice in order to retain any hope that he can influence the monstrosities that lie before him."

In other words, Freed believes that art can change society and, ultimately, (Wo)Man. This is radical, especially when you consider the fact that Freed lives in and writes out of a region of the United States that gave the world John Wayne, Charles Manson, Richard Nixon, and Ronald Reagan — and where the diminutive of radical, "rad," is an adolescent term for surfing.

He mixes Artaud — "the theatre, like the plague, is a delirium and is communicative" — with Socratic dialogue in order to create a "town meeting" collision of opposites. Debate is crucial, awareness a kind of victory: "The Theatre of Cruelty is surreal in one sense," he wrote in the "Inquest" introduction, "but this is balanced out against the torment of choice and freedom inherent in the will to survive the nightmare. To wake up is, in itself, an act of hope."

This aesthetic often pushes Freed's dramas into exaggerated, almost expressionistic, crises. Characters sing at the oddest moments, or cry out infantile gibberish when least expected. Suddenly a heroic figure drops to his knees and begs for understanding; in another moment, a society woman is grappling with pubescent neuroses. Class protects no one in Freed's dramas; Artaud's cruelty buries the critics who call it propaganda. His plays aren't didactic — they turn away from Brecht's Epic Theater. It's a theater of commitment.

Underlining every word — even the rather elegiac, romantic IS HE STILL DEAD?, about the last days of author James Joyce — is History.

"The coverup of the Kennedy murder amounts to a national scenario of lies and of fiction that drove America mad," Freed believes. "America, like Germany before it and Chile after it, became the name of a nervous disease. The leaders of the anti-war movement, of the Weather Underground, the Civil Rights movement, were bright young people who identified with John Kennedy and the Peace Corps, with the idealism of the early 1960s. It was the murder in Dallas, and then the blatant, transparent, vulgar cover-up, that soured a whole generation."

While Freed's critics condemn his work as being dogmatic, he's not above condemning Hollywood screenwriters' "false consciousness": "Writers always say their writing isn't going to change anything. It's not a message because you send a message through Western Union. It's not about an issue because plays about issues close on Saturday night. And on and on it goes: the aphorisms, the jokes, the disclaimers. It's all for money, it's all for entertainment, and therefore I could never get in trouble, never be blacklisted, never be hounded, never be imprisoned, never be murdered."

But during the Writer's Guild strike, Freed recalls, a "humorous" leaflet was circulated that read: "Why should we let producers hire someone else to turn into garbage what we can turn into garbage ourselves?"

"That takes your breath away because that reveals the opinion writers here have of what they're doing," Freed says, grimacing. "That's truly shocking."

Look around Freed's book-lined study and you'll not see a computer. Faithful to his classical preoccupations, the man writes by hand with a pen. "Writers these days keep saying to me, 'wait till you see my word processor'", Freed says with a laugh. "And I'm ashamed to tell them I don't even type, much less own a word processor."

So how can he be so prolific? "A tremendous energy is taken out of writers today who must constantly be looking for what will sell and what won't. This preoccupation has nothing to do with storytelling. The reason writers in the past didn't have what we call writer's block is because the concept of an original story was totally alien to them. Writing meant rewriting a received myth and body of communal stories. If you take our period from Dallas to Watergate to the great victory of Grenada, you have a period at least as rich as the Punic Wars or the Trojan Wars."

Freed's commitment to the politically conscious life is total, consuming even his social activities. Alongside his wife Patty, an old literary tradition is maintained in their home: the artist's salon. It is not unusual to be invited to a brunch or a dinner at the Freeds, then meet playwrights and producers, political organizers, actors and actresses, poets and musicians, even drama critics. The dialogue is invariably spiritied and literate. Instead of "how I got that deal" talk, these gatherings focus on more eloquent and lasting concerns. Pinter once defended an imprisoned political playwright it's now chic to praise, Vaclav Havel. At another salon, Julie Harris dramatically read Freed's monologue on Leo Tolstoy's wife.

Why go to the expense and trouble of mounting such events?

"We pay a terrific price, that we're not aware of, for not having cultural solidarity," Freed answers. "People don't work in groups, don't belong to a theater, there's no community of artists. So you have to put them together."

And so, through such salons, Freed has helped forge and link an international community of writers, political organizers, filmmakers and intellectuals. As the world's political consciousness rises with the fall of the Berlin wall and perestroika, as more artists follow Havel's lead, Freed's home becomes a crucial oasis for the Western front's gadflies and literary patriots, a kind of underground shelter for theatrical solidarity. It was Freed's political passions that initially attracted Pinter, whose own deep commitment to issues of censorship and torture further solidified their relationship. Such passions also made fast friends with actors Ed Asner and Lemmon. (Asner will be portraying the gadfly philosopher in a forthcoming Freed series titled SOCRATES MUST DIE! for Britain's television Channel Four.)

Pinter's relationship with Freed parallels his more overtly political works of recent years, especially "One for the Road" and "Mountain Language." In an interview accompanying the published version of "Road," Pinter explained the purpose of political writing for the stage in today's world: "All we're talking about, finally, is what is real? What is real? There's only one reality, you know. You can interpret reality in various ways. But there's only one. And if that reality is thousands of people being tortured to death at this very moment and hundreds of thousands of megatons of nuclear bombs standing there waiting to go off at this very moment, then that's it and that's that. It has to be faced."

You won't find a better definition of political theater. This anthology's three plays are about facing reality. Enjoy.

Memorandum

TO: DIRECTOR, FBI (100-449698)   DATE: 7/9/69

FROM: SAC, LOS ANGELES (100-71737)

SUBJECT: COUNTERINTELLIGENCE PROGRAM
INTERNAL SECURITY
DISRUPTION OF THE NEW LEFT

Re Los Angeles letter dated 6/17/69, and Bulet dated 7/1/69.

It is to be noted that the weekend of July 18, 1969, there will be a group meeting at Merritt College, Oakland, California, called "United Front Against Fascism in America" (UFAFIA). This group will be composed of members of the Black Panther Party (BPP), Communist Party, Progressive Labor Party and others.

In connection with the Cointelpro set forth in Los Angeles letter dated 6/17/69, and approved by the Bureau, 7/1/69, it is the thought of the Los Angeles Office that this will be a good opportunity to distribute copies of the throwaway indicating that DON FREED, one of the organizers of the Friends of the BPP, is actually an informant for a governmental agency.

For the information of the San Francisco Office, DON FREED is a Key Activist of the Los Angeles Office, who is definitely under suspicion by the BPP and other key activists, DONALD KALISH and IRVING G. SARNOFF. It is the desire of the Los Angeles Office to neutralize FREED by the distribution of a throwaway accusing FREED of being an informant. It is the thought of this office that the San Francisco Office could in surreptitious manner distribute

2 - Bureau (RM)
2 - San Francisco (Encls. 200)(RM)
3 - Los Angeles
    (1 - 100-67274)(DON FREED)
    (1 - 157-1618)(BPP)
jco/pjc
(7)

ALL INFORMATION CONTAINED
HEREIN IS UNCLASSIFIED
DATE 1/10/83 BY SP-3TAP/RB6

LA 100-71737

these copies at Merritt College during the UFAFIA Conference. Copies of this throwaway will also be mailed locally to selected individuals in the New Left Movement.

Enclosed herewith for the San Francisco Office are 200 copies of the throwaway "Don Freed is A Pig."

It is requested that unless the San Francisco Office is advised to the contrary by the Bureau, these throwaways be distributed, taking all steps necessary to protect the identity of the Bureau as the source of the leaflet.

San Francisco Office is requested to be on the alert for any information indicating the attitude of the recipients of this throwaway.

DON FREED IS A PIG

We don't know just what breed of PIG he is, but Freed is a LAPD PIG, an FBI PIG, a CIA PIG or maybe even a Sheriff PIG.....but he is a PIG, a lousy informant who deals with his fellow PIGS, and betrays us all.

The PIG as far back as 1957 while appearing at meetings of the Peace Action Council urged acts, these acts against the president when he appeared at Los Angeles in June 1967. He said he'd lead a group to comit acts of civil disobedience at Century Plaza.....the PIG wasn't even arrested.

Next, FReed urged mass draft card burning at the Century Plaza....the PIG never lit a match.

Freed urged the burning of Johnson in effigy at Century Plaza...and then he hid.

This doesn't convince you..especially our black brothers------Remember the anit-draft demonstrations in front of draft headquarters in Los Angeles.. everyone got arrested for blocking the entrance except the PIG, an the pig urged the sit-in.

Last month Freed spoke at the Huey Newton rally in front of the federal building and kept shouting, "We are All Panthers", We Are All Panthers" and urged everyone to protect the panthers..."with our lives if necessary"

Shortly after the rally the PIGS struck at the heart of the Panthers as our black brothers were arrested and beat.

AND WHO WAS IT TALKING TO PIG FREED JUST TEN MINUTES AFTER THIS RALLY???????????????

WE GOT NEWS FOR FREED*******PIGS WILL NEVER REPLACE PANTHERS.

All Power to the People

PLAYS BY DONALD FREED

ALFRED AND VICTORIA: A LIFE

ALFRED AND VICTORIA: A LIFE
© 1988 by Donald Freed

Dedicated to Gerald Hiken

ALFRED AND VICTORIA: A LIFE was produced by The Wilma Theater in Philadelphia, opening on 27 February 1990, with Blanka and Jiri Zizka as the Artistic/ Producing Directors. The cast and creative contributors were as follows:

ALFRED .... Jack Davidson
VICTORIA .... Bridgit Ryan

Director .... Blanka Zizka
Set design .... Andrei Efremoff
Lighting design .... Jerold R Forsyth
Costume design .... Maxine Hartswick
Additional design .... Craig Clipper
Sound design and original music .... Daniel Osterweil

Mise en Scene: The stage is space, broken by ramps, rises, and screens. Organic shaped objects — called "elements" — stand for chairs, chests, tables, beds, etc. Here and there are art objects, and there are small stacks of bound books. On the screens, images of the protagonists' lives and *our* times may appear between scenes. One element is a wardrobe wherein we see the costumes of the play: cowboy, Indian, Nazi, Vietnamese, nun, doctor, etc.

The action covers some twelve years (1968-81). ALFRED and VICTORIA age from 16 to 28, and 57 to 69, respectively.

ALFRED is a man of great wealth and power. Tan, expensively tailored, sensually handsome, athletically fit, his "Ivy League" accent and "phallic narcissism" mark his genus as: "American Strong Man — Late in the Age of Atoms — Now Extinct."

VICTORIA is a slim abstraction of American suffering. VICTORIA does not just play Beauty to ALFRED's Beast, nor is she merely the anima strangled in the intestines of male power. VICTORIA is a wonderfully graceful colt of a girl when we first see her, with an idiosyncratic, problematic, but authentic style and soul. This soul radiates through the lightning flashes of her neurosis.

Gerald Hiken's experimental first production in Los Angeles was enormously persuasive and profound. The *mise en scene* was a run-down, cheap nightclub. A dressing room, curtained off, occupied one corner of the stage, and the audience watched the actors change costumes between scenes. While this was going on, a "low-tech" radio narrative played featuring LBJ, Richard Nixon, R. Reagan, and other preachers and pundits of those years. Runners of lights bordered the ramp and the stage, and they flashed off and on as jokes emerged from the sound track.

Before each scene, a music hall-type billboard is changed to display the place and year of the scene.

PROLOGUE: THE AUDITION

(Dark. A spotlight. A voice from the rear:)

A VOICE: Next.

(Into the spotlight walks the awkward, adolescent VICTORIA. *Fearfully, she sings her song,* Multitudes.*)*

VICTORIA: I came to sing a song
And I will sing it now
And if I die tomorrow
Tomorrow will sing it for me
I came here
To be for all
(Echo)
And with all
And this song I sing
In my solitude
Will be sung
Tomorrow by the multitude.
(Spoken:) I wrote that myself.

A VOICE: Next...

ACT ONE

SCENE ONE: LOS ANGELES, AUGUST 1968

(The time-line: LBJ quits. RFK, MLK assassinated.)

ALFRED: Hi. Did Luther serve you champagne? — Good. Please, turn that off. Excuse me — Wendy is it? *(Off into a telephone)* Hello, Anna—

VICTORIA: Victoria. *(Lighting a marijuana cigarette)* "Hello, Anna." Anna Rexia, An-or-ex-ia... An "Anorexia Nervosa Journal." Dr. Siegel says I have to keep a journal and list everything I eat. Siegel says I'm not one, but I'm a "Potential". A "Potential", that's what my dance teacher at the Coronet said, and my English teacher and my.... Anyway, I had a chocolate shake with two eggs in it and, uh, yogurt.... Maybe I'll eat you, Dr. Jerry Siegel, because you're cute, your ass and all. I could eat you and get fat with child. That would cure the old anorexia, and it would kill my mother and that would cure the old nervosa.... (ALFRED *re-enters. They stare at each other.*)

ALFRED: What is that music? Did he give you hors d'oeuvres?

VICTORIA: What's your sign?

ALFRED: What?

VICTORIA: What's your, you know, birth sign?

ALFRED: Oh. Faeces.

VICTORIA: Pisces?

ALFRED: Faeces.

VICTORIA: I'm a "Moon-child". — You know what mine says for today? "Go to the most influential person you know to gain advice on how best to utilize your finest talents."

ALFRED: What is that music? Did you eat?

VICTORIA: The "Beatles." I'm not hungry.

(ALFRED *steps to pillar to talk on phone.*)

ALFRED: *(Nodding and muttering.)* Hello! — Hello, Anna. Yes... Tell her, about ten for dessert. What time is the Governor going to.... Go ahead — Go ahead

— Go ahead. Right, all right, go ahead — go ahead — go ahead... No. Thank you, Anna... Can we turn off that music? *(Music off)*

VICTORIA: Siegel says that if I don't watch out I'll wind up looking like a concentration camp victim. He says that no one can control their thoughts, so they try to control their bodies — he's right. Do you think he knows that I always had this fantasy of being chained up in a Nazi whorehouse?

ALFRED: Sit down... We met at....

VICTORIA: The Wilshire Club... I was modelling and —

ALFRED: That's right.... You're a model. You're thin.

VICTORIA: Not really... What kind of music do YOU like?

ALFRED: Classics: Beethoven, Bach, Cole Porter — anything but that *merde*.

VICTORIA: Oh... Well, I have a tape of *Hair*.

ALFRED: No thanks. Filth. Let's just chat for a few minutes... Where are you from, Vicky, is it?

VICTORIA: "Orange," California

ALFRED: Oh?

VICTORIA: It's true. I could say I was born in England... Let me guess about you.

ALFRED: Manhattan. Do you go to school? How old are you?

VICTORIA: Seventeen. I dropped out.

ALFRED: Can you read? Are you clean? What do you weigh?

VICTORIA: I'm clean. — Are you?

ALFRED: We take three baths a day. My friends and I.

VICTORIA: Together? Ha-ha... Good for you... Sounds like fun. Rub-a-dub-dub, three men in a tub... I read. My father made me memorize Shakespeare and the Bible. He was a great believer in the English language.... So I dropped out....

ALFRED: To model?

VICTORIA: Yes. No. I don't know.

ALFRED: Do you live at home?

VICTORIA: I — do you want one of these?

ALFRED: Marijuana? *(He declines, looks at his watch.)* You move very well.

VICTORIA: I'd like to write music and act if —

ALFRED: Stick to modelling. Let me see you move.... Go ahead... You're a natural.

VICTORIA: Plus, I'm not sure what to do with my talents.... Do you want to hear a song I wrote?

ALFRED: Just stay away from all the pansies and the little cloak and suitors that're crawling all over this town.... What are you, Episcopalian?

VICTORIA: How did you guess? Are you a Jew?

ALFRED: *(Laughs)* No... Christian Science.

VICTORIA: You are? I'm interested, what's the main idea? *(Hesitantly, she "models" as he talks.)*

ALFRED: Let me see you move. Go ahead... Christian Science? It's called "Science and Health".... Hold that, bend back a little...
"To preach deliverance to the captives of the senses
and recovering of sight to the blind
to set at liberty them that are bruised."
(He repeats this as he directs her, circles, touches her neck, holding her.)

VICTORIA: What does that mean?

ALFRED: Do you know the "dying swan" position? *(He puts her into the dying swan position. He holds her head down with his hand.)*

VICTORIA: I quit the church three years ago. *(Pause)* Have you read Kahlil Gibran? *(Pause)* I've got a cramp. *(He releases her, she sits on the floor.)*
I love Gibran. Do you want to hear the song I've done from it?

ALFRED: *(Long pause)* I have some things here I'd like you to model.
(He opens the wardrobe element and takes out a leather harness and riding crop.)

VICTORIA: Oh, do you ride?

ALFRED: No... Why don't you go in there and put this on. Go ahead, I'll get some champagne... or would you prefer, ah, popcorn? *(She stares.)*

VICTORIA: Mr. I don't even know your name, I —

ALFRED: Mr. Smith.

VICTORIA: Mr. Smith?

ALFRED: Go ahead, please.

VICTORIA: Listen, I'm not a real model, Mr. Smith.

ALFRED: Look, I can help you with your modelling or acting.... Go ahead, don't be a tease, little girl. You know why you're here. Now, do you want me to help you or not? It's getting late. *(Pause.* ALFRED *takes a $100 bill from his wallet and puts it on the table.)* One hundred dollars.

VICTORIA: Mr. Smith, I'm not what you think I am.

ALFRED: What "are" you, then?

VICTORIA: I don't know.... A rebel, I suppose.

ALFRED: A "rebel." How chic. Can you afford that pose? Against what, exactly, are you in rebellion? Or hasn't your psychotherapist identified the enemy for you yet?

VICTORIA: The kids on the strip are freaking out because they said they killed Bobby Kennedy, and then they killed Martin Luther King —

ALFRED: "They"? Both those men were murdered by jealous lovers, didn't you know that?

VICTORIA: No. You're making that up.

ALFRED: It's true. They were both whoremasters. Did you know that?

VICTORIA: The kids on the strip said the pigs killed them.

ALFRED: The "pigs"? Delightful. You call the peace officers sworn to protect you "pigs", and the gutter revolutionaries you call "flower children." Your acid dream of the world is charming, with its excremental ambience and its lingua franca.

VICTORIA: Plus which, I'm not a revolutionary. I'm not political.

ALFRED: Everything is "political." Just put these on and I'll give you a riding lesson. You need money, don't you? *(He takes his wallet out and puts another $100 bill on the table.)* Two hundred dollars. Now, go ahead. Two hundred dollars.

VICTORIA: Mr. Smith, I need money, but I promise you I don't know what you want me to do.

ALFRED: Oh, Christ, get out, then. What are you, a virgin, for God's sake?

VICTORIA: Do you know the story of the Virgin by Kahlil Gibran? — We had to learn it for English. Well, you be the knight; use that riding crop for your sword. I'll be the virgin, the nun in the monastery. He's going to rape her. *(She kneels before him; he holds the crop.)* "Oh, fierce knight, this salve, if you rub it on your body, will protect you from the blow of the sharpest sword." — Then the knight said, "Amazing, let me see it, for, in truth, I fear death." — "Terrible knight, see I will rub it on my neck. Take your sword and strike my neck with all your might. Strike, dread knight, strike!" *(She offers her neck to him. As if in a daze he pantomimes striking with the crop.)* The nun's head rolled from her body. She had saved her virginity.... And the knight went mad and ran from the monastery weeping like a child, "I killed her! I killed her!" *(She rises. ALFRED stares at her.... He is moved. Now ALFRED kneels at her feet. VICTORIA stares in panic.)*

ALFRED: Again.

VICTORIA: What?

ALFRED: Don't be afraid. You've heard of S & M? Sadists and masochists, slaves and masters, the whipper and the whipped. Well, the truth is, the whipper is the slave and the whipped is the master. Go ahead. *(He mimes the role of the nun as she repeats the story.)*

VICTORIA: "Oh, fierce knight, this salve, if you rub it on your body, will protect you from the blow of the sharpest sword." Then the knight said, "Amazing, let me see it, for, in truth, I fear death." "Terrible knight, see I will rub it on my neck. Take your sword and strike my neck with all your might. Strike, dread knight, strike!" *(She strikes slowly. He falls. She cradles his head as if it had been severed.)*

ALFRED: You have talent. You have...something. You shouldn't be here. Twenty years ago I could have done something for you — when I was, ah, producing.

VICTORIA: You were? Films?

ALFRED: Theatre. I could have done something for you, then.

VICTORIA: Is it too late for me, do you think?

ALFRED: I don't know....

VICTORIA: I love the theatre. I was in *Our Town* once.

ALFRED: In the legitimate theatre you have to be a priestess, not a whore.

VICTORIA: I know. *(Drops her pose)*

ALFRED: In Greece the actors were priests, in Rome they were whores.

VICTORIA: And in Hollywood —

ALFRED: Whores.

VICTORIA: Did you know Marilyn Monroe? *(Pause)*

ALFRED: Why?

VICTORIA: I don't know. I feel for her.

ALFRED: You feel for her?

VICTORIA: Why not?

ALFRED: — Do you want to be a priestess or a whore?

VICTORIA: — I don't know. Is that all there is?

ALFRED: Let me see you act the role of a thoroughbred colt. Go ahead, it's your audition. *(She dances out a colt improvisation. He joins her.)*

VICTORIA: — Why did you stop?

ALFRED: It's a long story.

VICTORIA: Why did you stop the theatre?

ALFRED: A friend of mine gave me the advice — "Close the show and keep the store open nights".

VICTORIA: What store?

ALFRED: Umm? Oh, nothing. My family. They had a store once.

VICTORIA: Oh. What do you do now?

ALFRED: Nothing. Philanthropy. Nothing... "Leisure industries."

VICTORIA: What's that?

ALFRED: Resorts... Fun.

VICTORIA: Fun?

ALFRED: Organized fun.

VICTORIA: ORGANIZED fun?

ALFRED: Very... What do you "do"?

VICTORIA: Really, nothing.

ALFRED: Then you're nobody. *(Pause)*

VICTORIA: That's true.... But I will be....

ALFRED: Will be what?

VICTORIA *(Very softly)* I will be.... I will be me. *(Pause)*

ALFRED: You're blushing.... You're a character.... You've made pornographic films, haven't you?

VICTORIA: One. I was starving.

ALFRED: But you like the "starved look", don't you? How long have you been a...in the *demi-monde*?

VICTORIA: I beg your pardon.

ALFRED: In the "Life." The LIFE.

VICTORIA: The "life"?... Oh... French, I studied Spanish.

ALFRED: It's a barbaric language. A friend of mine, Senator, ah, says they make good pickers because they're built so close to the ground. *(She begins flicking riding crop.)*

VICTORIA: Who said that?

ALFRED: Never mind. A friend of mine. Are you going to put these on or not? It's getting late.

VICTORIA: We're not communicating very well, are we? I think that's important, don't you?... You don't live here do you?

ALFRED: No. It's a *pied a terre*.

VICTORIA: Did you study French?

ALFRED: Yes.

VICTORIA: Where?

ALFRED: Yale... What's it going to be? You want more money?

VICTORIA: We passed through New Haven. It's beautiful. What did you take there?

ALFRED: Business administration and classics.

VICTORIA: Classics! Faust? Right? *(He agrees.)* Who's your favorite author?

ALFRED: Sade.

VICTORIA: Sade?

ALFRED: The Marquis de Sade.

VICTORIA: Oh... Yes, I've heard of him.

ALFRED: You have? What have you heard?

VICTORIA: Oh, you know... sort of "randy," my father would say. How old are you?

ALFRED: I'm young enough to be your father. Do you like that? The Marquis de Sade was a great writer. "...Swear to me that I shall one day be your victim...."

VICTORIA: Go ahead.

ALFRED: "Since the age of fifteen my mind has been ablaze, obsessed with the idea of perishing, a victim of libertinage's most cruel passions...to become, in expiring, the occasion of a crime is an idea that makes my head spin...."

VICTORIA: Beautiful writing.

ALFRED: Go in the other room now and wait for me. Go ahead. We're going to have a play. I will call you Justine, and you will call me, ah, "Daddy Smith"...go ahead. *(Pause)*

VICTORIA: — Yes.

ALFRED: *(Shaking)* "For out of the heart proceed evil thoughts".... Who are you, child?

(ALFRED *counts out a pile of money. He drops it down like falling leaves on* VICTORIA, *who has knelt down to pick up a bill. The money floats down, in the spot-light, covering* VICTORIA.)

SCENE TWO: LOS ANGELES

(The time-line: Kent State shootings. Secret bombing of Southeast Asia. Black Panther slaughters.)

(A blackboard reading "To be read for this week: Anna Karenina, Madame Bovary, Hedda Gabler. *For Discussion 12/23/70 :* King Lear*")*

ALFRED: — Ah, *King Lear.*

VICTORIA: *King Lear.* How sharper than a serpent's tooth it is to have a thankless father.... Ha, ha? No. *King Lear. King Lear* is the tragedy of a father who, umm, who can't umm, accept true love. King Lear is not Santa Claus and he is not old Father Time — he is Cordelia's father but he is really her child — "I had thought to make my rest on her kind nursery" — remember? But then he comes in at the end with Cordelia in his arms — "Howl, howl, howl, howl!" But she's really HIS mother, AND Mother Nature, AND Mother Earth! It's like yesterday I read that Mother Earth is the labyrinth, right? Raped by Theseus, right? And the Queen of the Amazons — that's Hippolata, right? That's *Midsummer Night's Dream*, right? And the King of the fairies was also the King of the Fairies. *(*ALFRED *protests.)* Wait! Wait — there's more — Freud? Freud said that "in every man's life there are three women". King Lear had three daughters.

ALFRED: NO! STOP! *King Lear* is the story of a KING. King Lear is a KING. His daughter Cordelia loves him, truly, and he loves her — but that's beside the point.

VICTORIA: Love is not beside the point, love is the point.

ALFRED: Love is beside the point! Power is the POINT, and PROPERTY! Cordelia wants to marry the king of FRANCE. France! And Lear is not about to give up a third of ENGLAND to the fucking king of France.

VICTORIA: You mean —

ALFRED: I mean it was all a provocation. They set Cordelia up!

VICTORIA: No, she said "nothing" when her father asked her what she had to say.

ALFRED: It didn't matter what she said or didn't say. He was the king of England and it was his job to hang on to every rocky inch of it, and to fuck the king of France.

(They laugh, and sing.)

ALFRED & VICTORIA: "How could Red Riding Hood have been so very good and still kept the wolf from the door?"

VICTORIA: Al, you are the vulgarest Marxist of them all!

ALFRED: And you're a capitalist dupe. *King Lear* is about property, and love has nothing to do with it! What do you say to that? *(Pause)*

VICTORIA: "Nothing". *(She runs to embrace him.)* You're a king, but if you tried you could be a father — a wonderful father! *(She covers him with kisses.)*

ALFRED: What's the matter with you? Are you stoned again?

VICTORIA: *(Kissing him)* You're not my father! So, stop it! — You're the father of my child. I'm pregnant. *(Smiling hopefully)*

ALFRED: How? *(Pause)* I'll have you sent to Puerto Rico for an abortion. — I have to fly down there anyway next week for the "Rockefeller Conference on Population Control." *(Pause)* What is it, kid? You have to have an abortion, you know that. You know my situation. Besides, you don't want a child, now. Bringing a child into this madhouse? You don't want that....

VICTORIA: There's something in me that wants to be born. I don't know how to say it.

ALFRED: Say it.

VICTORIA: Something you gave me that I want.

ALFRED: Poor Vic.

VICTORIA: Let me have it. Please, Al.

ALFRED: You'll make yourself sick, Krazy-Kat. You can't get blood out of a stone, Vic.

VICTORIA: I can. I did. I got blood from the stone. From you. *(She attacks him; he pins her to the floor.)* If I can't have it, then you cut it out. Now! With your own hands.

ALFRED: Don't ever try and make a man like me feel guilty. Not if you want to live.... *(She starts to leave.)* What are you doing? — Where are you going?

VICTORIA: To have my baby.

ALFRED: How will you live?

VICTORIA: A job. I can get one.

ALFRED: You? Where? Doing what? What do you want to be, kid?

VICTORIA: Someone that...

ALFRED: Go ahead.

VICTORIA: That...you...don't...want...me...to...be.

ALFRED: Like who?

VICTORIA: I don't want to be Anna K. lying on the tracks, under the wheels of the 5:13 — poor Anna. Don't wanna be Emma B. with the black bile pouring out of her mouth.

ALFRED: No.

VICTORIA: Or Hedda G. with her father's pistol up her nose —

ALFRED: God, I love your mind — what I've made of it....

VICTORIA: Don't want to be Madam Butterfly or Madam Bovary, Anna, or Emma, or Hedda, or Jane — I don't want to be killed!

ALFRED: You have a mind! You could be —

VICTORIA: I could be Vickie or Cindy or Candy or Wendy or Dawn in bed with your opposite numbers in Vegas or at the Springs. Look up, Mr. Smith, see that person up there? — That's me up there, looking down on the last two years of this fuck-film you call my "Liberal Education."

ALFRED: That's not fair.

VICTORIA: You've been shoving your "Old Masters" down my throat for two years, but I'm still alive. My baby and I are alive and we are not alone. *(She reveals an underground newspaper.)* See: jobs, places to crash, clinics, legal aid, *(Weeping)* aid, mutual aid...

ALFRED: I warned you never to bring that filth into my presence. I won't have that rag on the premises!

VICTORIA: These are my people. These are my "classics."

ALFRED: You are going to Puerto Rico, or you're going to an asylum.

VICTORIA: No I'm not — I'm going back to the street. *(Reading from the newspaper)* "Dominant Bitch Goddess Mistress Vee commands all slaves to come and have their asses whipped!"

ALFRED: Boring!

VICTORIA: There's your "Science of Mind" by fucking — Mary — Baker — fucking — Eddy! *(She hurls books.)* "Call Aunt Rose, she has that high colonic for you that the Doctor ordered. Night or day." You don't need me. You can have it both ways, Al. You can have Mrs. Eddy and Aunt Rose in your stinking private sector. You don't need me, you're not interested in me, or anything I have to offer. I'm leaving, and I'll survive, because if no one buys my songs then I'll just get out and hustle right along with "Fiona", and "Sexy Showgirl", "English outcall", "She-Mate", and good old "Tie me —

spank me." — And thanks to having been tutored in the "classics" by great men like you, I'll be a star! You'll read all about me in the underground press.... *(Her voice sinks.)* You know what the worst is — you've never once asked my permission for anything! Just stay here with your classics and send for "Candy", or "Liberty", or "Tie me up".

ALFRED: Have you lost your mind?

VICTORIA: I lost it, you found it, and you burnt a hole in it with your money, and now it's all soft wax and brand names.

ALFRED: So boring — like all the others.

VICTORIA: Yes, you're so fucking sensitive, such great heterosexual gentlemen — all of you great Palm Springs gangsters and whoremasters. Your pornographic poolside poker parties. Pimps and procurers, pinching and pinching — flacks, hacks — ex-presidents leering, war-criminal comedians shmeering — and there you are the king of Palm Springs, cheering on your palace guard of Fortune 500 child molesters — and there in their cabanas, your wives, the little women — drool in the pool — winking and stinking — singing the praises of their proud princes.

ALFRED: Vickie, I'm warning you —

VICTORIA: My fucking ass. What do you know about anything except fucking the whole world in the ass. You ought to get down on your knees and KISS the ass of the whole human race. *(She breaks down, unable to leave or stay.)*

ALFRED: I don't know whether you're completely out of your mind on dope or the town's greatest actress. But understand this, wage slave: It's my kind that do the work of this country. We create the system and the wealth. We are reality and you are shadows. We live, you exist. We hold up the Ramparts of Freedom. We meet the payroll! THIS IS THE FUNCTION OF THE RICH! From now on I owe you nothing. I could chain you here if I wanted to or I could kill you with my bare hands. I'm strong. My friends and I are strong. We have to be to keep that scum out of our linen closets and our nurseries. We're strong and we're getting stronger every day. I'm waiting.

VICTORIA: For?

ALFRED: What for?

VICTORIA: Oh... "No, no, please don't — oh — please — sir..." *(Getting on her knees)*

ALFRED: I give, you take. I diet, you starve. I live, you die! That is the theory of the Wealth of Nations, and I am THAT THEORY IN THE FLESH! See, look at my body, look at my health and strength. *(He "models" now for her.)* I'll give you one more chance, pot head. You get that little ass down to

Puerto Rico tomorrow and get fixed. And when I get there, you'll do what I want and with whom I want and you'll beg for more. And you will read three classics by next week. Three! Because I am the book and you are the bookworm. When I get to Puerto Rico you will tell me the story, in detail, of *Don Quixote*, *The Red and the Black*, and the *Prometheus*. And you will memorize the role of Io. A little nymphomaniac cunt like you who tries to steal a big man — like me, BIG — away from a goddess. Well, that's you — Io — and that's me, Zeus, the lightning bolt!... I owe you nothing. You owe me — and my friends, that you despise so — you owe me your SOUL. I can get all the bodies I want out there on the street — there's a nation full of bodies out there for the taking. We don't need your stupid bodies. You're dead. As of today, you're dead and your soul belongs to ME! *(The lights fade on the ritual. The music and news report of the time line come up.)*

SCENE THREE: ATHENS, AUGUST 14, 1974

(The time line: Nixon quits, American complicity in Chile, Greece, etc. revealed. OPEC crisis.)

*(*ALFRED *stands in his spot, dictating into the telephone.)*

ALFRED: Anna, I want this hand-delivered to the President at the Winter White House.... Dear Mr. President and Pat, I want you to know that our thoughts are with you today in your hour of crisis. It has, literally, made me physically ill — your treatment. If it were not for the fact that B. is in Paris and I've just arrived in Athens we would have been at LAX, to greet you.... Here in ancient Athens, in Ted Agnew's friend's superb villa, I am moved to consider the ways of power and time. You and I have discussed tragedy and time, Mr. President — how well I remember your remarks in Florida on one sad occasion. Last night we — make that "I" — I attended a performance of *Prometheus*. I could not help but think of you as the Titan's torment was played out.... Paragraph and, uh, ask about Trixie and the family, etc.... Close with this: Ah... I hope you know how painful this all has been to the Governor and those of us close to him and how despicable the rumors in certain Washington circles have been. Of course the Governor will not dignify such slime with a response. However, he assures me that he and Bill and Ed will be in regular contact with you during this, the transition period.... Ah, uh... In the years ahead I know that the nation you served so loyally will right the wrong called "Watergate".... Right this wrong and, ah...that history will record you as one of our greatest presidents, a man of peace and a man of vision.... Uh, Anna, see how that reads, if it's too smarmy, you edit, will you? — Send his wife a piece of jewelry, something inexpensive but get it in New York, not Beverly Hills, and wrap it in plain brown paper and have our messenger hand it in person to the president, as if it were a covert transaction. In other words, Anna, make it look like a bribe — to cheer him up, you know, because the Governor's people tell me that he's already made two attempts on himself and that she's become a dipsomaniac, so it's important to pep them up if we can. Thanks Anna... Oh, my, ah, travelling secretary is here, but I'll do any business through Staris Brothers. So far as V. is concerned, you don't know where she is.... Thanks again, Anna, I'll be home in about ten days, it's so hot here that I'm sick.... Anna, don't tell anyone that I'm sick. Ah, book me into the Harkness Pavilion under an assumed name, Smith will do, for the week of August 1st. Call Doctor Rohauer... There's an item in a column in the *International Herald Tribune* that I'm going in for a triple bypass. Knock that down hard, Anna, if that son-of-a-bitch from *Fortune* magazine calls. The market's going mad in the OPEC crisis, anything could happen, so tell Stanley to sell short —

(He is wracked by a fit of coughing. He is perspiring. He takes several pills. In silence we hear the sea and sea birds. He closes his eyes and stands immobile. From time to time — as VICTORIA *speaks — he twitches or mutters as if in a nightmare.* VICTORIA *slips into her spot and talks into her telephone. She is in sandals and a simple white dress.)*

VICTORIA: Athens is incredible! The colors, the sea, the people. We're in a heavily guarded villa but still I feel something here that I've never.... I feel I could be, well, not happy, here, but that I could find.... No, not happiness, but, ah, joy? And the food — I can't stop eating — the food is the stuff of life: aveolemono, and moussaka, of course, and stifado, katifa, and bougatsa and cafe daki. Shhh, mmm... We've been to see *Electra* and *Prometheus*. They made me come! They knocked me down...Alfred, too. The *Prometheus* wracked him — awful sobs of some buried agony.... "Agony" — I have a Greek tutor every morning — "Agony" as in agon, as in a wrestling match. Not those fat fakes on T.V. but two beautifully muscled men wrapped in each other's arms on the red attic clay — oh, Jesus — I know I could write if I could stay here. But he won't, he's got some kind of flu and he has to meet his family in Phoenix for some.... He's not the same man, he's so sad, and we never have sex. I don't mind — give me catharsis.... But he cried when the girl with the horns came on and stared up at Prometheus lashed to his rock.... "What country, what race have I reached? Who is this that I see lashed to these rocks?"...I could act, I could write!... Alfred says that the Greek colonels are going to forbid the playing of the classics. He had an argument about it with the man who owns this place. — Something about "torture on Mikonos".... I've never seen that side of him before. I mean, where he would put *Prometheus* above the colonels — I could have hugged him.... He's a strange man, he's so down since we got here, and I am so high. God, I'm high on tragedy! Tonight we see the *Oedipus*. "E-the-pus" — sore foot, he who walks in pain. God, I can't stand it —...I choose Ithaca,

Mediterranean thought, balance, sanity, and the generosity of those who understand.... I don't want to waste any more of the life I have left....

(ALFRED *coughs, collapses.* VICTORIA *murmurs something and hangs up.* ALFRED *appears, looking at* VICTORIA *as she exits. When she is gone,* ALFRED *exits after her, mouthing her name; he has had a stroke.*)

END ACT ONE

ACT TWO

SCENE ONE: BEL-AIR, CALIFORNIA, DECEMBER 23, 1976

(Time line: Carter elected; "Committee to Elect Ronald Reagan", and "Moral Majority" formed and merged.)

(Darkness. Moonlight. Exterior of ALFRED's *Bel-Air castle. We see a stone terrace, wide balustrades. French windows, u.c., closed — lights dimly lit inside. Far off, the sound of a marching band. Enter* VICTORIA, *in sweat shirt, jeans, and backpack. She crawls up the ramp toward the balcony. She pauses, listens to night noise and music, then she produces a pea shooter and shoots a volley at the glass doors.* ALFRED *appears with flashlight and revolver. She lofts another volley of peas, they rain down on* ALFRED's *gray head. He stares up at heaven in wonder, she chuckles, "Pantalone". He gasps. They find each other, she is on the balcony in his arms. A slow, serious kiss.)*

ALFRED: I was so lonesome for you, Vic. Six weeks.

VICTORIA: I tried to get in.

ALFRED: I know. She..."she" had Maurice and his gay Gestapo around the clock. Next time — I've arranged it with Anna — I'm going to St. John's. I trust the nuns.... Don't ever have a heart bypass.

VICTORIA: O.K.

ALFRED: And don't ever go to that pain palace of a Mount Hebron Hospital. It's Kafka. I was in the Meyer Lansky Memorial Wing, that's just south of the Jack Ruby Intensive Care Unit. It makes me very happy when you laugh....

VICTORIA: What do they say about your heart?

ALFRED: That it's broken.

VICTORIA: That's "schizophrenia" in Greek. "Schiz" — broken —

ALFRED: You're getting good.

VICTORIA: Next year, Homer.

ALFRED: Champion... If I had a heart I suppose it would be broken.... Whole country.

VICTORIA: What?

ALFRED: The whole country has a broken heart. Schizophrenic. Whole country.

VICTORIA: Umm. Whole world. *(Laying out backpack snacks)* Fuck. I dropped the popcorn. Here's the champagne. *(They start to laugh.* ALFRED *freezes.)*

ALFRED: Shh. I think he's down there.

VICTORIA: Who?

ALFRED: Maurice, the spy.

VICTORIA: Maurice, the spy?... I thought Maurice was your male nurse.

ALFRED: He is, in theory. But the new boy in the poolhouse, Humphrey, tells me everything. He's a Yalie.

VICTORIA: Al, Al, is this a lunatic asylum? Double-agents and "house dicks"! *(They scream with silent laughter.)*

ALFRED: Shh, don't, I'm not well —

VICTORIA: I know, but you're not crazy.

ALFRED: They're crazy.

VICTORIA: They're crazy. *(She stuffs food in his mouth.)*

ALFRED: God, this tastes good. But, I can't, I'm fat as hell.

VICTORIA: That's crazy, Al, you're no fatter than I was. Your jogging'll kill you.

ALFRED: *(Trying to exercise)* I know. It's male anorexia. I did it in four feet of snow and in 100-degree heat in Miami. All of us, the Secret Service trotting like dogs at our heels.... Some black kid hung over the side of a fishing boat and sang out — "Why the fuck don't y'all run after Justice!"... That stopped me....

VICTORIA: Shh. I think I hear someone.... I guess not. Umm, good. Have some more.

ALFRED: Not now. You never stop. No more anorexia?

VICTORIA: No, I've joined the great oral majority. Life tastes good. And you, señor?

ALFRED: Well...our little tea party.

VICTORIA: Yes. I'll be the, uh, uh — what is that word? — Oh, yes, "mother." That's who I'll be. How's the old Ataraxia?

ALFRED: Please don't speak Greek.

VICTORIA: Without, you know, passion.

ALFRED: Oh, that. Yes. Well, the flesh is willing....

VICTORIA: It is?

ALFRED: Your flesh, I mean. Your body. Your bawdy body.

VICTORIA: What about yours?

ALFRED: Mine? Me? A bad case of "heterosexual panic."

VICTORIA: They're leaving. Stay down, Daddy Warbucks.

ALFRED: They're going out. I could die here, and they're on their way to the Marina to disco. I could die here.... Change the music now, I'm getting depressed....

VICTORIA: What's that music?

ALFRED: One of those filthy bands from UCLA.

VICTORIA: My God, why're they practicing football music at Christmas? Isn't their season over?

ALFRED: Never. It's never over.

VICTORIA: Al, put your feet up. Feel the air, feel the breeze, Al, and the flowers — that wisteria, those roses....

ALFRED: I wouldn't know. I've never been in the garden, in all these years. It makes me nauseous.

VICTORIA: "Nauseated." THEY'RE "nauseous", YOU'RE "nauseated."

ALFRED: I feel like throwing up, O.K?

VICTORIA: I'd like to be buried there — that's where the bodies are buried — and come up lilacs.... Look at the dirty old man in the moon, Al. Breathe. Ahh, just to live! To live! I'm your doctor, tonight. Here, this is "Rolfing."

ALFRED: Well, I'll be bound. What is it?

VICTORIA: Very ancient.

ALFRED: Very fake... Feels good, but harder, come on. You've got hands like Jesus. Need, k-nead.

VICTORIA: This, we call "Holistic Therapy"; no, stay on your back. Now, make any sound you "feel". (VICTORIA *straddles* ALFRED *and massages.* ALFRED *growls and moans throughout, making them both laugh.*) Shh. Of all the therapies, I like this, because it can, uh....

ALFRED: Lead on to love making. Yes, with anyone but me.

VICTORIA: That's premature, a bit, isn't it.... What's that? (ALFRED *pulls the flashlight out of his pocket.*)

ALFRED: Sorry. Let sleeping dogs lie, Vic, it's better.

VICTORIA: My poor old Marquis de Sade can't take it anymore. — Maybe it's physical.

ALFRED: You're right. That's probably why I'm afraid of sex — that it'll kill me.

VICTORIA: Have you ever known a night like this?

ALFRED: Yes! Around 1935. I was eighteen or nineteen, a sophomore at Yale, not yet "tapped" for Skull and Bones, not yet corrupted beyond recall. I was very young, maybe not much older than you were when we met. "We're in the Money" — and the bright boy of the Drama Club. And a virgin — I lied about it to the others, but I was. And my masturbation had reached epic proportions: there I was, the budding, black-haired satyr clutching that pitchfork penis of mine; wearing out couches, beds, desktops, my right hand, my left hand — inseminating the surface of all inanimate objects from New Haven to Boston and back again to New York; the Johnny Appleseed of the Northeast corridor. Erotomania and bliss in the linen closets of Fuckminster Hall or wherever I lived and died in those onion skin years of my rite of passage from the universe of my hand to the other orifices of this world and, I have no doubt, the next, seeing as how I am a true believer and born-again God-fucker!... But to return to our tale of legendary lust: There I was, in a brown cashmere sweater, bent double by blue balls brought on by the thought of Miss Evangeline, that proud and only daughter of none other than my own Dean of Classics. How many times I had raped her in dreams, repeatedly raped her until she begged for more. Yet even then in my perfect ignorance I knew that any crime was better than love. One fateful midnight, I met Miss Evangeline in the flesh! I was walking out late at night, looking for a tombstone to masturbate on. It was a dark spring blackness. Grinning my grin I stumbled through the gates of the cemetery and under the arch that reads, "THE DEAD SHALL RISE". — Stumbled past the crooked, crazy-angled grave tablets with the names — Pierce and Puce and Blair and Blore — and all the names of the mighty Yale dead.... And stumbled over Miss Evangeline herself where she knelt at the sinking foot of her ghostly, ghastly, groping godfather's grave. There, then, in the spying moonlight, young Alfred, impaled on my arrow of longing, knelt and stared into the violet pools of the eyes of the kneeling Evangeline.... You say — "Alfred? Why Alfred, what are you doing here?"

VICTORIA: Alfred? Why Alfred, what are you doing here?

ALFRED: That's it — and I say, "Did I step on you?" *(They act out the dream of young love.)*

VICTORIA: "Hurry, Alfred, before the night watchman comes along. Do you want to touch me? No one ever has. There. And there. Yes."

ALFRED: "Yes. Yes. Here. And here. It would be wrong, but it's wrong not to, isn't it?"

VICTORIA: "Don't stop. Why are you staring like that? Are you going to kill me or love me?"

ALFRED: "I don't know.... If you got pregnant?"

VICTORIA: "Then I'd be full of life, and clean."

ALFRED: "Or full of death." *(They fall slowly out of their assumed characters.)* I'm getting sleepy. *(Pause)* There are signs of life around the pool house.

VICTORIA: Any around here? *(She checks his crotch again.)*

ALFRED: Forget it. It's no use.

VICTORIA: What do men want?

ALFRED: Let's go to South Africa —

VICTORIA: Let's go back to the Greek Islands —

ALFRED: And we'll get a heart transplant and —

VICTORIA: I'll get a new head or —

ALFRED: No, wait, — I'm serious. We'll go and they can put a new one in. You think?

VICTORIA: Black.

ALFRED: I don't care —

VICTORIA *(Overlapping)* An old black woman's heart.

ALFRED: Are you giving me a second opinion?

VICTORIA: Sure. A wise old black woman.

ALFRED: I've tried everything else.... Or we could have sex and die right now, before the return of Maurice and Clytemnestra. Except that I can't.

VICTORIA: It's now or never Alfred. Make me pregnant and I swear I'll stay out of your pants, more or less permanently. — You owe me one, kid.

ALFRED: You don't want a baby now! In this madhouse?

VICTORIA: Don't tell me what I want. I know what I want! I'm through being Mrs. Smith. I want to come in the front door. I'm giving myself permission to be "legit."

ALFRED: That's what they all want. That's what Marilyn Monroe wanted. She forgot her place and they put her in it.... You asked me once, remember, whether I knew Marilyn Monroe. I knew her. We all did: Jack and Bobby and Jimmy and Frank, Abe and Harry and Ronnie and Al.... I was in Sy Gold's office when she signed her ten million-dollar contract. She signed her name, she looked around that office at all of us, and she said, "Gentlemen, I have just sucked my last cock." She wasn't signing a contract... she was signing her death warrant. You don't understand. You never have. Do you know what they would do to you after I'm gone, if you had my baby? That's property! Remember King Lear!

VICTORIA: I love you Al.

ALFRED: Love is beside the point. Property is the point. Power is the point. My wife and the governor would put on their spike heels and slice you to ribbons.

VICTORIA: Al, stop.

ALFRED: We're Skull and Bones, skull and bones, skull and bones: souls that can't be quoted, faces not for attribution; watch out for us, kid. We cut off our noses to spite our race. — Ha! Our motto is — PRIMUM PUELLAE ET FEMINAE, "Women and Children First". If you're rich, you hire Henry Kissinger to do it — if not, Charlie Manson. And I bought it wholesale because I was the heartbreak Jew-boy with the cleanest linen and the dirtiest money.

VICTORIA: Do you tell all this to your shrink?

ALFRED: Of course not. You think I'm insane? My therapy's the moral equivalent of jogging.... You tell yours the truth?

VICTORIA: I try.

ALFRED: *Naif.* These bastards would've had Joan of Arc on thorazine. Shh! That IS someone in her room. Hide!

VICTORIA: Shh. *(He turns out the lights. Complete darkness. Silence.)*

ALFRED: I want to say something.

VICTORIA: What?

ALFRED: About what you said before. I know that you are my true wife in the eyes of God and I want you to know that I know what I did.

VICTORIA: What?

ALFRED: I know what I did. *(Pause)*

VICTORIA: Al, I'm not Beauty, and you're not the beast.

ALFRED: *(Sound of sobs)* Yes, I am. We are.... I molested your soul.

VICTORIA: Don't say that, Daddy. *(Silence. They sing a sad refrain of* "How could Red Riding Hood....")

SCENE TWO: CHAPEL, ST. JOHN'S HOSPITAL, SANTA MONICA, CALIFORNIA, AUGUST 1981

(The time line: Ronald Reagan's "creative society" in place, secret war and rumors of war)

ALFRED: Forgive me, Father, for I have sinned. Mea culpa, mea culpa, mea maxima culpa. I reject the devil and all his works. In the name of the Father, and of the Son, and of the Holy Ghost, amen... *(He makes sign of cross, wipes perspiration from brow.)* Ahh, Father, I, ah. I am — as we discussed — I am in the process of, uh, washing my hands of the Atlantic City situation. I don't care what it costs me — because I know it would be wrong. *(Makes sign of cross)* Uh, the Phoenix, mm, deal is still a problem because Mr. D'Angelo's mother is involved but I absolutely intend to liquidate it by the first.... *(Sign of cross)* Now, ah, Father, I ah, — I've told you everything about my life and my wife, and, ah — Victoria.... And, yes, I remember everything you've said about, ah, "cleaving" to my spouse and nuclear family, but, Father — and I don't want the fact that I'm building a hospital, for your order, to influence you — but, in my heart, Vicky — Victoria —is my true and only wife. She is in my heart forever as I hope to forever be a part of the sacred heart of my Lord and Savior, Jesus Christ.... *(Sign of cross)* Please don't say anything now, Father — but if I could just take a meeting with you and the Cardinal, I'm prepared to make him a firm offer and the hospital and the college are below the line and completely separate from the question of who my true wife in Christ is. Let me put it another way: In 1946, we had a merger of.... *(He drops his voice in secrecy.)*

SCENE THREE: LOS ANGELES, CALIFORNIA, AUGUST 1981

(Lights up on VICTORIA, *talking)* — Hold it right there, Dick. You're his lawyer, you drew his will, you — just a minute. You know that Alfred wants me to — no, I don't want — to hold, tell the other person to hold — Dick — I get the books and records, I get the paintings from the other house...yes.... Go ahead, go ahead... Oh, no! I don't care what it costs to sue all of em! I'm talking to a publisher — never mind "Who" — I'm, I'll get the money.... That's right.... You better believe it.... Your fuckin' A... Go ahead...Dick — I think you may be developing a tiny conflict-of-interest here between your client and your neck and your ass.... Well, that's what I think and unless you convince me otherwise — I'll handle it myself.... You got it, Richard — Portia and Shylock and the "quality of mercy"! and I'll get back to you! *(*VICTORIA *hangs up, pauses, sips champagne, then she dials another*

number.) Hello, Anna. Anna, this is V. No, not B., V. I want to get a message to Al at St. Johns. Are you ready?... Dear Al, I received your letter and the legal document. Thank you. I was very moved. It was very generous, and be assured I will kill to keep all the books, paintings, records, etc.... As to your wish to be buried in Greece: I'm consulting Dick Kline as to the legal options.... I think I know why they have you in the hospital under a false name with no visitors permitted, and why the White House keeps saying that you're "recuperating in Palm Springs". Al, know that I will take care of myself, whatever happens.... Whatever happens, we'll be buried next to each other in the red ground of Greece.... Time will pass and we'll catch up to each other, and the gray-haired father will lie with his mad daughter, at last. And you will rise, at last, and from our bodies, underground, will grow the wild, coarse Greek grass of life.... Anna, thank you. *(*VICTORIA *hangs up. She exits. Music up.)*

SCENE FOUR: ST. JOHN'S HOSPITAL, SANTA MONICA, CALIFORNIA, AUGUST 1981

(Swaggart and Reagan on sound track. VICTORIA *enters in a nun's habit.* VICTORIA *runs toward* ALFRED*'s intensive care unit. A small crucifix hangs in the air above* ALFRED*'s bed.)*

VICTORIA: Al, it's me, the "fighting nun." I bribed Sister Mary and Maurice.

ALFRED: Mother of God.

VICTORIA: Jesus, Al, shh. We don't have much time. Al, do you know me?...

(ALFRED *is delirious, slipping in and out of consciousness. His voice is that of a dreamer: rapid, low, charged.)*

ALFRED: — Huh? Uh. Uh. Uh... I know you. I know you — you're the Cardinal's man.

VICTORIA: Al, shh, listen...

ALFRED: Don't hurt me. I'll pay, I'll pay anything. My wallet, get my wallet — oh, God, they've stolen my wallet! The Communists stole my wallet and the Cardinal told 'em to do it.

VICTORIA: Shut up, Al — they'll hear us.

ALFRED: Help!

VICTORIA: Al, stop, listen — it's me — see? "I came to sing a song", remember? Al, I've come to say good-bye. Do you know me?

ALFRED *(Whispering)* Sister? Sister — take a message to the Cardinal: Tell him I burned the tapes, no one can touch him now. I flushed 'em down the terlet. I have the proof, it's in my wallet. The tapes are in my wallet, the money's in my wallet, everything's in my wallet. —But, listen, Sister, come here, don't show the Holy Father the Trojan in my wallet, don't show him the rubber. I never used it, never. Show him the money, and Sister, listen, you take some — yeah, yeah. You take some too — buy something for yourself — Sister, promise me you'll take my money, promise me — *(He repeats the above in Italian.)*

VICTORIA: Al, shut up — wake up. *(ALFRED tries to get under her habit, as he talks in English and Italian.)*

ALFRED: Com'ere, com'ere — what's under there? Gotta know what's under there. Is my wallet under there — you're sitting on it goddamit let me have it. *(ALFRED struggles and curses, sings and laughs.)* Give me Communion, I want the flesh and blood of my Lord and Savior Jesus Christ! *(VICTORIA puts ALFRED's wallet in his mouth.)*

VICTORIA: Crazy old man. Crazy old bundle of secrets. *(ALFRED freezes.)* You're not a Catholic, you're not a Christian Scientist, you're not even a Jew. You only ever believed in money. You were born with money in your mouth: You studied it, you worshipped it, you married it, you elected it. "Homo Erectus Americanus — late in the age of atoms — now extinct". Those hundred-dollar bills I crawled for, all those years ago — the compounded interest on those hundred-dollar bills fills up every bank in the world.... So, Mr. Smith, "S" is for suffering, and "M" is for more suffering— and with these bonds I thee wed. *(She sings and ties him up with his belt.)*
How do you do my partner.
How do you do today.
Will you dance in a circle,
If I show you the way....
(In a reversal of Extreme Unction, VICTORIA begins to administer the last rites.)
The nurses, the nannies, the tutors, the coaches. *(Beating)* The doctors, the lawyers, the teachers, the captains. *(Beating)* The brothers, the buddies, the kitchen, the cabinet. *(ALFRED arches in extremis. VICTORIA chants her invocation.)*
Who are these women?
Who are these women?
Who are these women?
So cool and
So thin and
So blond and
So dumb and
So grateful
WHO ARE THESE WOMEN?

ALFRED: Victoria!

VICTORIA: THEY ARE NOT ME, ALFRED. They are not me!

ALFRED: Victoria. I HAVE RISEN! *(She gets into bed and mounts him.)*

VICTORIA: Give me your seed, monster.

ALFRED: Victoria!

VICTORIA: No charge. It's over.

*(*VICTORIA *strips off her nun's costume, sings a few phrases of her first song,* Multitudes. *The lights fade to black on the tableau of* ALFRED *and* VICTORIA. *We hear the news reports of their deaths, and the rising sound of the news ticker.)*

*(*ALFRED*'s death:)* ...The multimillionaire member of the President's "kitchen cabinet" died today in St. John's Hospital in Santa Monica.... A spokesman for the hospital stated that the patient had been checked into the intensive care unit under a false name but refused to....

(Ticker sound rising)

*(*VICTORIA*'s death:)* ...was bludgeoned to death in the early morning hours... the former model was the mistress of a powerful advisor whose death two years ago led to a court battle involving....

THE END

CHILD OF LUCK

CHILD OF LUCK
Copyright © 1990 by Donald Freed

For Laird Williamson

CHILD OF LUCK was originally produced by the Denver Center Theater Company, opening on 1 May 1989. The cast and creative contributors were as follows:

JOHN THOMPSON KELLY II	Jamie Horton
COUNTESS VIRGINIA DE TOLEDANO	DeAnn Mears
REVEREND BILLY HALE	Jim Baker
PATRICK D THOMPSON	Archie Smith
STEVEN KATZ	James L Lawless

Ensemble: John Clark, Kay Doubleday, Carole B Elmore, Mitchell Hudson, Merrill Key, Blayn Lemke, Kendrew Lascelles, Percy Howard Lyle Jr, Jeffrey W Nickelson, Ken Allen Robertson, Steve Wilson

Director	Laird Williamson
Scene and costume design	Andrew V Yelusich
Lighting design	Charles MacLeod

CHARACTERS

JOHN THOMPSON KELLY II, the 39-year-old congressman, heir to a great American merchant prince.

COUNTESS VIRGINIA DE TOLEDANO, widowed mother of JOHN T KELLY II, now married into Spanish nobility. Age 73.

REVEREND BILLY HALE, evangelical leader of extremist religious groups and a presidential candidate. Age 50.

PATRICK D THOMPSON, great-uncle of JOHN T KELLY II, former advisor to JOHN KELLY senior, and liaison to the White House. Age 87.

STEVEN KATZ, chief advisor to KELLY. Age 65.

WASHINGTON HEWITT, black revolutionary and presidential candidate of the People's Party. Age 40.

CONSTANCE CONRAD, former mistress to JOHN KELLY senior. Age 63.

ANCHOR PERSON

News people, police, crowd, KELLY aides

Note on Crowds

The choral action of the crowd should only be suggested: for instance, by letting the actual audience in the theater represent the mass of people; by using a wide range of positioned speakers, off-stage, to project chants, bands, riot—to make the mob "obscene" off-stage. Toward the end of the play, where shadowy figures are required, the candidate's "entourage," and the "Press," can fill these roles.

In summary, the *mise-en-scene* is designed so that as few as eight principals and a company of as few as four or five will be sufficient.

Time: January 2000

Place: Old City Hall, Chicago

The elapsed time of the action is from three pm until eight at night.

All the action takes place on the steps and in front of old Chicago City Hall, and in two enclosed adjacent areas.

The old City Hall is a massive neo-Roman structure that fills up the stage: stone, marble, and huge columns. The two Press Rooms are situated left and right of the sprawling steps and plaza of the City Hall. They are entered through heavy double doors. Or, the media booth may be a suspended glass bubble with a map of the world as its environment.

The street and space in front of the City Hall steps is occupied, on this bright winter afternoon, with Police who have roped off the speaker's area on the steps. The media contingent is pressed up against the ropes and crowd control barriers. Sirens and helicopter chopping rise and fall. The wind blows, clocks chime.

The rest of the space, off stage, is seething with competing religious and political activists, of all races, and a fraction of the vast homeless population of America in the year 2000. Posters and banners proclaim: "Kelly for President", "America Needs Another Kelly", "Kelly in 2000". Other signs, of the religious extreme, predict apocalypse brought on by sexual and political corruption: "Americans Against AIDS (AAA)", "Communism =AIDS", etc. Still other slogans can be seen calling for "Peace and Justice", etc.

Skinhead guards surround REVEREND HALE. The air is heavy with pollution. AIDS victims pass through, looking like Holocaust "survivors". Police, wearing yellow rubber gloves, roam the edges of the stage.

(In the darkness, before the curtain, can be heard the building street sound of the crowd, the police, the media, including: The REVEREND BILLY HALE, *leading his followers in the singing of* "Give Me That Old Time Religion"; *the revolutionary* WASHINGTON HEWITT, *urging on his backers in the anthem,* "Are You Ready, Nigger?")

(From out of the rush of the crowd cacophony, the voices of the MEDIA *slowly register and dominate. Still in darkness:)*

FIRST MEDIA VOICE: ...to announce his candidacy. The thirty-nine-year-old son....

SECOND MEDIA VOICE: ...World Cable News has learned that the late John Kelly's widow—now the Countess de Toledano—has arrived from Spain to stand at her son's side when he makes....

THIRD MEDIA VOICE: ...to sources close to the candidate, Congressman Kelly will announce his "America in the Twenty-first Century" plan to deal with the—quotes—"continuing crisis of health, homelessness, and war that now plagues the American people...."

(Lights up. POLICE, *off, hold back the crowds as media people report the scenes into their cameras and microphones. Off stage, a band strikes up* "Happy Days Are Here Again". *All turn to see* PLAINCLOTHES AGENTS *running across the steps, followed by the candidate,* JOHN THOMPSON KELLY II, *and a group of* POLITICAL NOTABLES, *featuring the candidate's uncle, former mayor* PAT THOMPSON, 87, *in a wheelchair.)*

(The CROWD *roars, cheering and booing; the* POLICE *react; the band plays. In the eye of the storm stands* JOHN KELLY: *athletic, handsome, no overcoat, his shock of brown hair startlingly like his father's. He looks out over the scene, then waves and points to supporters, then gestures for silence, and steps up to the microphone. Finally, silence; the* MEDIA *crouch.* KELLY's *words echo and bounce off the buildings.)*

JOHN: ...Mayor Thompson, Alderman Carbonara, Congresswoman Warsawsky, Senator Greene, members of the City Council here today—my fellow Chicagoans, my fellow Americans: Before leaving for Washington and the official opening of "Campaign 2000", we wanted, I wanted, to stand here on these steps, in my home town, here where my father stood in 1960, shoulder to shoulder with the young John F. Kennedy, my godfather. You remember; you've all seen photographs and paintings and dramatizations and documentaries of that famous moment when my godfather, the candidate, John Kennedy, announced his "New Frontier" — and my father, the young John T. Kelly, pledged that corporate America would lead the way to that New Frontier. *(Cheers)* There they stood: The brightest and the best, Kennedy and Kelly, Boston and Chicago, forging the partnership that would become legend....That day, the soon-to-be-president called on my father to speak, and my father said — you've all read and heard the words — "America has more than a future, America is the future." — And then John Kennedy said, and I say it today, "I intend to offer myself for the office of the presidency of the United States!" *(The* CROWD *now erupts. Waves of sound roll in from offstage; from what would be the surrounding streets. There is also heckling and hostility. The* MEDIA *maneuver, dancelike, and the* SKINHEADS *prowl.)* John Kelly, my father, was a great speaker. I am not. His was the human face of capitalism. Many of you remember or still see him on television. He said in 1961 — when he became the first director of the "Freedom Corps" — that there were "two Americas — rich and poor...." (CROWD *reaction)* And that brings me to what I want to say, in my own words, about the "crisis and the challenge" — as he called it — that we face here and now in the year 2000. — The challenge of the twenty-first century, and the reason that I am running for president of the United States, is to tell the truth, to confront the connected crisis of poverty, health care, and war. — I say "connected" because the impact of each —

(The RELIGIOUS FANATICS, *under the* REVEREND HALE, *begin to chant.* WASHINGTON HEWITT's MILITANTS *respond against them.)*

VOICES: *(Off, echoing)* Quarantine! — Quarantine! — Quarantine!

(Off, the POLICE *force apart the contending and chanting contingents. Sirens.)*

VOICES: *(Off, echoing)* Justice! — Justice — Justice!

JOHN: ...and there has been a "quarantine" since 1998. And with great doubt and misgiving I voted for it. — Let's tell the truth! *(Screams of outrage)* I voted to put anyone testing positive for any sexually related disease into a "quarantine setting." The congress voted for it — and the president signed it into law — and not only has it not stopped our disease crisis, but it has opened the door for the round-up or arrest or quarantine of thousands of people —

(Off, the POLICE *struggle with a near-riotous* CROWD. *Sirens.)*

POLICE BULL HORN: Clear the area! — Clear the area.

(The POLICE *drive the extremists back to the edge of the stage, left and right, giving the candidate more space and scope for his declaration. Noise continues, off.)*

JOHN: — our environment, our health care and social welfare systems, are breaking down — some will say have broken down — and there are voices raised to fix blame, to find a scapegoat, to blame everything from our farm crisis to the catastrophic drought across the heartland—to our savings and loan and stock market disasters, to the burning of our embassies across Latin America—all this, some want to blame on racial groups, and religious groups, even on sexual groups who are accused—

VOICES: *(Off, echoing)* Queer—queer—queer....

VOICES: *(Off, echoing)* Kelly—Kelly—Kelly....

(An eruption of fury, off, brings the POLICE into the CROWD, again, clubs rising and falling. A REPORTER is injured. A helicopter hovers, a VOICE from the sky.)

VOICE FROM HELICOPTER: This will be declared an unlawful assembly and you will be placed under arrest unless order is restored....

(Slowly, the mob subsides, under the blasts of electronic noise.)

JOHN: Remember! Remember who we are! Men like my father and President Kennedy were able to harness America's industrial might to put a man on the Moon. Today, I promise you that I will organize a war on this plague that is now being called "The American Disease". I promise you a new commitment. Sealing our borders has not worked; mandatory abortion for mothers who have tested "positive" has not worked; making all sexual intercourse outside of marriage illegal has not worked; and quarantine has not worked! *(CROWD chants.)* I understand—I understand your frustration and anguish. That is why I am here today: to remember together—to tell the truth together. Truth is our platform in this election. *(Cheering, chanting, "Kelly—Kelly....")* In the days to come—in the days to come, I will be laying before the people of the United States detailed proposals. Proposals that address our dying economy and its cancerous debt. *(Cheers)* But first of all, I intend to declare war on that complex of fatal diseases— *(Cheers starting)* starting with AIDS— *(More cheering)* that has reached into millions of American homes—of every race and class—that has caused our brave people to panic—our young people to refuse to marry and start families, and yes, even to touch each other, and to pit the races, the religions, the classes—Americans all—one against the other! My father and President Kennedy stood here and called to you—"Give me your hand!" That was forty years ago, one year before I was born. Today I say, "Give me your hand"—not just to integrate schools in Alabama, or put a man on the Moon—great as those feats were—but I need your help to rebuild America—our ruined farms, our war-zone cities—homeless America—give me your hand!

(The black radical leader WASHINGTON HEWITT snakes past security up onto JOHN's step. As the POLICE move to stop him, HEWITT interposes PAT THOMPSON's wheelchair between himself and the POLICE and GUARDS. The old

man in the chair signals the security to back away and let HEWITT *talk—for a minute.* HEWITT *is deep-voiced and mature, in the style of Malcolm X.)*

HEWITT: Call your guard dogs off, Kelly—I'm not hijacking the wheelchair—the Mayor, here, is going to live forever—so call 'em off, and let me have three minutes on national TV.—You made the choice to come into the street and talk to the people—well, welcome to the street.—Now, you gonna let me have my chance before they anoint you king?

JOHN: *(Pause)* Don't hurt him!

HEWITT: Look, Congressman, I'm not looking to hurt anyone—I have something to say that you need to hear—now, do you have the guts to listen to the ghetto, because I'm speaking for the "niggers under the mud", and the bloody rags that're left of the "Rainbow Coalition"!

(HEWITT's *followers begin to sing*—"*Are you ready, nigger—you better get ready....*" HEWITT *signals for quiet.)*

JOHN: *(Pause)* Move away from the chair. *(Pause)* Okay—say it.

HEWITT: You and I are the same age.—My middle name is Kelly—after your old man. My real name is George Washington Kelly Hewitt. Ain't that pitiful.—And, now, here we are.—You think you're going to the White House, and they want to take me to the "big house"—they want to put me into jail for "conspiracy to riot". And you're the liberal mask the hangman's going to wear when they declare the "state of national emergency"—let me finish, now!...When you declare it. Because this is America, where a liberal named Kelly's going to be "elected" to pull the plug on democracy....
Well, chump, here's the message from the grassroots: When you get to the City of Lies—the so-called District of Columbia which has been locked down for two years—when you get there and they throw up the bodyguard of lies around you—remember this: We're out here in the cold waiting—in our millions—waiting for justice. We want an accounting and we want it now, or we're going to burn this Babylonian motherfucker down, block-by-block—by block! Hold on! We want the people in the Pentagon, and the CIA, and the DIA, and all the rest, who created the AIDS virus, who let that killer out of the biological warfare test tube—brought to justice! (CROWD *reaction)* That's right! Like they developed the LSD and the rest of that shit that lobotomized our fathers before us. *(Crowd)* And brought in the heroin from Southeast Asia in the sixties and seventies, and the cocaine from Latin America in the eighties, and strung out a whole generation—we charge genocide! *(The* CROWD*)* So, you've got to choose, now, Kelly! Join us and face the people who ruined this country and killed your President Kennedy, and Martin Luther King, and your father—and every other decent man of his generation—or try to wipe us out yourself—join us or kill us—

(In the uproar, PAT THOMPSON *runs his wheelchair straight into* HEWITT, *from behind his back, and knocks him down. The* POLICE *leap on* HEWITT *and carry him off. At the same time, other* POLICE *beat the mob back, leaving* JOHN KELLY *shouting.)*

JOHN: No! No violence. Let him go! — I promise you I will not bring charges. I promise you! *(*THOMPSON *is wheeled out by aides.* KELLY *fights for control of the throng.)* Remember who we are! We don't have to be afraid. I'm not afraid! — Not afraid of desperate voices of any extreme, Left or Right. *(*JOHN *moves into the* CROWD/ AUDIENCE, *touching, shaking hands, even embracing people. He is winning them over.)* The world has always called the United States of America a lucky country. The poet Robert Frost, at President Kennedy's inauguration, called America "the gift outright". America had the rich open land, the mineral resources, the waves of hard-working immigrants — America had all the luck. And, I, too, the son of a Merchant Prince, grandson and nephew of mayors and governors, with the best education, the best of everything this nation has to offer — I know what it is to be lucky...and what it feels like to be unlucky.... We have that in common — each one of us — we have all had some bad luck. Some have said that our luck turned bad when my father and President Kennedy, ah, died — but I don't believe that. The truth is that the American people made their own luck, and though I've had every advantage and every good break, I've worked hard and I've made my own luck. That's the truth! And by working together again, starting now with this election, all of us together can turn our luck around again and finish my father's unfinished agenda! *(The cheering builds again.)* So give me your hand and we'll turn our luck around — the luck of the Kellys, the luck of the Irish, the luck of America!

*(*JOHN KELLY *is lifted up onto the shoulders of the crowd. The band and chorus sing out "Strike Up the Band!" and "Happy Days Are Here Again".* KELLY *is paraded up and down and around. As the procession exits, all break into the campaign song: "Kelly", sung to the tune of George M. Cohan's "Mary".)*

CROWD: "For it was Kelly, Kelly, long before...."

(The square is empty. POLICE *keep the* HEWITT *and* HALE *followers pushed offstage. They can be heard in the distance. Street cleaners enter to begin clearing the strewn steps and square. The big city hall bell tolls as the sounds dim and the lights cross-fade to one of the press rooms.)*

(This "Press Room" is actually a "high-tech" media studio. The REVEREND BILLY HALE *is being interviewed by an important* NETWORK ANCHOR *in this gleaming cockpit of cosmic news. The interview quickly explodes.)*

REVEREND HALE: ...He backed down before that terrorist. It made me physically sick to see that terrorist — and you media people went along with it! And the Kelly kid kissin' his "you-know-what", and daring to say that the greatest country in the history of the world is dying of "bad luck"!

ANCHOR: I know that you have said that it is "God's Will" that has brought America, in the year 2000, to, perhaps, its most dangerous situation. You —

REVEREND HALE: —More dangerous than the Civil War, or the world wars, Lord have mercy! More dangerous than the threat of Soviet invasion. And it's not "God's Will", it's the Devil's Work. And John T. Kelly the Second is doing that work today as surely as his father was in 1963 when the Devil claimed his own. You see, we know that—

ANCHOR: Excuse me, excuse me, Reverend Hale, this is not the first time that you've referred to Congressman Kelly's father and family as somehow —

REVEREND HALE: As corrupt! Not "somehow" —And I challenge him, Kelly, to —

ANCHOR: What do you mean? "Corrupt" how? You're a candidate for the presidency yourself...you're the founder of a new party, the Family Party, and Congressman Kelly challenged you today to—

REVEREND HALE: Look at you, ready to die to protect the good name of the Kelly Klan, just like you always—

ANCHOR: Will you answer the question—isn't it true that you're —

REVEREND HALE: You save your questions for John T. Kelly the Second—

ANCHOR: I'm asking you—

REVEREND HALE: Or watch me destroy him in the debate! Praise God!

ANCHOR: *(Pause)* What debate?

REVEREND HALE: *(Rising)* The debate that I'm challenging him to, right now. Amen.

ANCHOR: When?

REVEREND HALE: Now.

ANCHOR: Now?

REVEREND HALE: You heard me. Right now. Right here. Hallelujiah!

ANCHOR: What makes you think that Congressman Kelly will debate you, today?

REVEREND HALE: Because if he don't—we're going to give the public the truth about the Kelly family—and he won't be here to answer....

(In the pause, the REVEREND *hands the* ANCHOR *a leaflet, smiles into the camera. Lights cross-fade to the other Press Room, opposite. This is not a media studio but, rather, a plain meeting room with a table, chairs, TV set, coffee bar, etc.* JOHN KELLY *and* AIDES *enter and watch the TV coverage. We can hear, but not see, the*

television screen. KELLY *and his group are high, excited, "winners". The action begins with the last speech of the* REVEREND HALE *from the preceding scene.)*

REVEREND HALE: *(On TV)* "...Because if he don't — we're going to give the public the truth about the Kelly family — and he won't be here to answer....

(KELLY *and all freeze. Silence.)*

ANCHOR: *(On TV)* One moment, Reverend. We have to take a commercial break. We will return to this, the third day of the first year of the twenty-first century, the third millennium, the first and already violent day of "Campaign 2000". World Cable News facilities are available to you, Reverend Hale, and of course to Congressman Kelly. The Reverend Billy Hale, the leader of the Family Majority, has just issued a challenge to John Thompson Kelly, the Second, the young congressman from the Seventh District of Illinois, and the son of the late Chicago tycoon.... Here is a 1963 clip of father and son on the beach, just days before a bomb exploded and killed —

(KELLY *turns off the TV. All talk and congratulate each other. Then an* AIDE *brings in snacks. Coffee is poured, etc. The* MEDIA *are barred physically.* KELLY *speaks to a beautiful female* ASSISTANT. *Sirens and street sounds in the distance.)*

JOHN: Is her flight on time? *(Hugs her)* We're on a roll! Is she here?

ASSISTANT: It's his new Ajax, they're coming into the, uh, that special, uh —

JOHN: The Executive Strip —

ASSISTANT: That's it, at —

JOHN: At Midway. Did you get my Uncle Pat out there to meet her in the —

ASSISTANT: "Mediacade". Right, again, Boss. — By the way, you were magnificent out there.

JOHN: How can anyone so sexy, be so smart?

ASSISTANT: I declare, I was just going to ask you the same thing. Seriously, you were "presidential".

JOHN: I'll tell you my secret —

ASSISTANT: You will?

JOHN: Sure. Later.

ASSISTANT: *(Exits)* Promises, promises. Later — Mr. President!

(Laughter, then strategy, led by the cigar-smoking chief advisor, STEVEN KATZ. *The pace is charged.* KATZ *wears thick glasses and speaks like a New York machine gun.)*

KATZ: Jack — the media — there's going to be a feeding frenzy when your mother and Uncle Pat get here, so don't let them talk — bring them straight in here, before they go to the hotel....Where is the good Reverend Hale at this moment in time?

(A SECURITY AIDE with an electronic extension is in one corner of the room. Three telephones are in use.)

SECURITY AIDE: He's still in the WCN studio waiting to debate the congressman.

JOHN: Shirley, tell them I intend to meet with Reverend Hale in a public setting, after I've talked to my mother and uncle.... Steve?

(The pace is almost frantic, overlapping speeches.)

KATZ: I agree. Wait a minute, Shirl. — Now, you handled Hewitt — it was "presidential". You turned it around. But Hale.... The polls show that every time Hale attacks you or your family or the Kennedys it improves our position. *(To an aide)* Leo, tell "World Scope" it's tomorrow.... But — see, look at these readings — but at the same time, the same polls tell us that the public — over sixty percent also believe that your father's death, the rumors, uh, family problems — whether you're Prince Charming or Alexander the Great —

JOHN: That cigar is as old as all these rumors. Gahd, it stinks.... *(To an aide)* Hi, let's see. Hah! *(To KATZ)* Look, my father, as far as the country is concerned, was Prince Charming and Alexander the Great —

KATZ: Except for those who were jealous of him and —

JOHN: And hated him. Right. Look, if these were normal times, I would never even acknowledge Hale's existence, but —

KATZ: Exactly. You have to confront him, you have to destroy him — in public. Today. Like you did Hewitt.

JOHN: Today! I thought you meant in a debate later in the —

KATZ: No. That gives him too much credibility. He'll "sound-bite" us to death. It has to be today. Short and sweet, as if he were a heckler, a drunk.

(JOHN and KATZ talk through the incessant activity and telephoning of aides.)

JOHN: *(To an aide)* I can't.... But he's paranoid, there'd have to be ground rules. With Hewitt I had no choice, and I was lucky, but with —

KATZ: No. Excuse me, Jack, but that's not good enough! *(To an aide)* He said he can't! — Look, the polls show that the public loves you, but they doubt whether you're tough enough to handle the bomb throwers of the Right like Hale, or of the Left, like Hewitt. So, that was good, very good out there. But, they need to know that you're the man your father was — as they remember him.

JOHN: *(Pause)* Could you all excuse me and Mr. Katz for a few minutes? — Thank you. (AIDES *exit.*) ...What are you saying? Lay it out.

KATZ: *(Pause)* Okay.... Your father was "capitalism with a human face". He ran the Freedom Corps!

JOHN: Yeah.

KATZ: Then, after he died, over the years....

JOHN: Yeah.

KATZ: People published raw sewage about, you know....

JOHN: His sex life — yeah.

KATZ: Well, according to the in-depth polls — and I mean in-depth — the sex stories and gossip secretly only underscored their perception, the public's perception, of your father as a man. A big man.

JOHN: With testicles.

KATZ: Exactly.

JOHN: And now? I mean after all this time, a female vice-president —

KATZ: Yeah. Still...this country is in a panic. They want a man on a white horse. So the fact that you've never been touched by any scandal — at all — is a mixed blessing.

JOHN: You mean because I don't play around.

KATZ: You're perfect. You're "Honest John". But....

JOHN: But I'm not married. And I'm discreet.

KATZ: True. So people question whether you're tough enough to deal with this situation.

JOHN: So?

KATZ: So, you have to take Hale on — right now — on national television, and it's got to be rough. They want "Reality", "Real-Time" TV. The public wants action, not rhetoric.

JOHN: *(Furious)* What am I supposed to do, rent a wife and one-and-a-half children, and shack up with two-and-a-half movie stars? — Your polls! You've been telling me that every poll since 1996 says the same thing — that the American public now believes that sex equals disease, AIDS, and that celibacy is the "g'damn wave of the future" — your words — that the country wants "a g'damn saint", isn't that what you've been telling me?

KATZ: But that was before!

JOHN: Before what? We've been running up to today for four years — and it's always been the polls and the pundits and the prophets and the oracles want me because A — I'm a Kelly, and B — I'm clean! Now you say "before" — before what?

KATZ: *(Pause)* Before Hale and his "Family Majority" started this. "The Kelly Curse!" — Don't laugh. *(He hands the candidate a memo.* KELLY *reads in silence. More noise, off.)* It's not funny.

JOHN: Not remotely.

*(*JOHN *reads, shaken. Finally* KATZ *goes to* JOHN *and gives him an embrace.)*

KATZ: You see what I mean....Either they destroy you with this, or....

JOHN: I destroy them.

KATZ: Either — or.

JOHN: How? — How do you answer this kind of "big lie"?

KATZ: Sex.

JOHN: No.

KATZ: Hardball. — Wait, let me finish. We have files, we have film. They have lies, "disinformation" — we have facts, on film. We have "choir practice"!

JOHN: Go down into the gutter?

(Their voices rise, again.)

KATZ: That's where they are —

JOHN: And what about the country —

KATZ: And that's where power is.

JOHN: *(Pause)* In the gutter?

KATZ: In the sewer!

(From off, there is an upsurge of noise, then a pounding on the heavy doors.)

AIDE: *(Off)* Your mother's here....Congressman, she's here.... *(*JOHN *and* KATZ *are still staring at each other and the "Curse" memo.)* Congressman?...Steve? — The Countess de Toledano, she's here.

(The door swings open. JOHN *hides the memo.* BODY GUARDS *flank the doorway. The aged man of 87, the man who knocked* HEWITT *down,* PATRICK DOWLING THOMPSON, *florid and famous, is wheeled in. He is* JOHN KELLY's *great uncle, a former presidential advisor and mayor. Only his magnificent white-haired head and voice have retained their aura and resonance.)*

THOMPSON: Jack!

*(*JOHN *kneels to embrace him. The old man whispers hoarsely to him.)*

JOHN: Uncle Pat. Are you all right? — You saved the day.

THOMPSON: It was like the old days. The old team. You and me, Jack, we're going to win, again. Win-win-win!

(The old man gasps for breath. KATZ puts out his cigar.)

THOMPSON: *(Whispering)* Be kind to your mother. *(In a normal stentorian tone.)* God bless you, Son, we need you. The country needs you! *(To an AIDE)* Let the Cardinal in as soon as he gets here.

(More GUARDS, offstage, break a way through the MEDIA, and VIRGINIA DE TOLEDANO, the COUNTESS, JOHN's mother, reaches the doorway. Seventy-three, strikingly chic, lean and still raven haired, with New England accent and the timbre of a great actress.)

COUNTESS: Johnny.

JOHN: Mother. *(They embrace, rather stiffly, to a barrage of flashing cameras from the corridor, off. JOHN starts to step back, but the COUNTESS holds on to give the MEDIA more photo opportunities. Finally, she releases her son.)* Well, thank you for coming — you look marvelous. You never change.

COUNTESS: No.... By their masks ye shall know them.... Johnny, can we clear the room?

KATZ: *(Pause)* Ladies and gentlemen, thank you, thank you very much. *(Shouting into the corridor as he moves people.)* Thank you very much — the Countess, and the Candidate, and Mayor Thompson will all be available to you on the steps in two hours — six o'clock, on the steps, that's a promise —

(KATZ is swallowed up in the MEDIA mob. The big door slams behind him. The uproar recedes. Mother, son, and uncle are left alone.)

COUNTESS: Johnny, you look champion! I've heard all about this morning. Champion!

THOMPSON: Wonderful. A home run.

JOHN: Well, so do you.... Uncle Pat saved the day.

COUNTESS: *(At the snack bar)* Pat, do you want anything?

THOMPSON: I don't mind if I do. — That Mau-Mau, Hewitt, he's not so bad.

COUNTESS: Black and beautiful.

THOMPSON: Yeah. Some day we might even wish we had him back again....

JOHN: Mother, let me pour that. Agua minerale?

THOMPSON: Give me a real drink.... Be careful.

(He points to what could be a surveillance ceiling device.)

COUNTESS: Balls! Every time I come home, you point toward the ceiling! You look like Michelangelo's talent agent. *(They all laugh.)* You can't live that way.... If they tap your telephone and wire your bed, that's their problem.... I say "they" — I don't even know, anymore, who "they" are, here.

JOHN: Mother — thank you — for coming....

THOMPSON: *(Breaking the tenseness; pause)* "They"....Well, I'll tell you one thing — they make us old-timers look like a choir of pantywaists.

COUNTESS: What a singular, old-fashioned idiom.

THOMPSON: It's the God's truth. They're all tied in with the radicals and the dope dealers.

COUNTESS: *(Laughing)* That is rich! — Just look at Johnny.... *(They stare at* JOHN.*)* Look at that noble brow. Inherited directly from your father, "Hizzoner" Big Bill Thompson.

THOMPSON: *(Laughing, to* JOHN*)* Your mother is the funniest white woman in the United States of America. *(As she anatomizes her son, the* COUNTESS *indicates portraits of former Chicago mayors that dot the walls of the room — also, the picture of John Kelly, Senior.)*

JOHN: Mother, it's late...the media.

COUNTESS: They can wait! I did not fly eight thousand miles to return to my native land to have people point to the ceiling and tell me to watch out or "they" would get me. — I expect my son, the next president of the United States, to protect me from "them". — Now, then, notice his Big Bill's brow. And, ah, those shoulders — what a hunk! — if that isn't "Hizzoner" Michael J."Boss" Kelly, his paternal grandfather's coal miner's neck to the life....
To say nothing of his father's sharp blue eyes, that shock of hair, and those long, strong fingers. — I mean, the boy's a gene machine — three generations of political heavyweight champions. Schooled by you in all the craft and cunning Chicago has to offer. You dare to suggest that he can't protect me from this local rabble? Balls!

THOMPSON: *(Laughing)* Bravo!

JOHN: Mother.

COUNTESS: This current clutch of little men who may or may not be spying on my son at this moment. My son — the heir apparent to all this pride and power. *(She gestures toward all the photographs and portraits. Silence.)*

THOMPSON: You know, Virginia, I always said that you should have been president.

(They all smile.)

JOHN: It's true....But did you notice, Uncle Pat, she didn't point out anything about me that I inherited from her?

COUNTESS: Who is "she"?

JOHN: What? — You.

COUNTESS: From me? — I'll let you know. If you win the presidency.

THOMPSON: Yes, indeed...I think we better talk about that — it's getting late.

JOHN: The evening news deadline, and that goddamn debate.

COUNTESS: What do you want me to say? — I don't think I should actually say anything....

THOMPSON: Well....

COUNTESS: Do you? — I mean, I'm here, I've come over from the "Old World". I've been a private person now, for years and years.

THOMPSON: Jack?

JOHN: I don't know. How long do you plan to stay over?

COUNTESS: I don't. I want to get back.

JOHN: Working on the "big" book?

COUNTESS: Yes.

THOMPSON: I can do all the talking.

(A sound of a band in the distance)

COUNTESS: But of course.

JOHN: *(Pause)* Mother....

(She smooths her son's hair.)

COUNTESS: How are you? — You look wonderful.... Do you want this, Johnny — do you have the fire in the belly — do you really want to be the "Man"?

(JOHN *smiles and takes her hand.*)

THOMPSON: The country wants him.

JOHN: Do they?

COUNTESS: *(Pause)* What about this religious con-man of the "cloth", "Reverend" Hale?

THOMPSON: What about him? He's a phony.

COUNTESS: He's a clown. That's what we think in Europe.

JOHN: What else does Europe think?

THOMPSON: Who gives a good goddamn.

COUNTESS: *(Listening to the band)* "Chicago, Chicago...." — We think, they think that the United States has had a nervous breakdown, and they want to know, "Who lost America?"

THOMPSON: They can go to hell.

COUNTESS: A complete breakdown. Again.

JOHN: What do you think?

COUNTESS: Well, when you put ten thousand people on an Indian — what do you call it?

JOHN: A "Hygiene Reservation".

COUNTESS: A "Hygiene Reservation". "Family Majority"! My God, whatever happened to the English language? Well, when you do that, people all over the world scream "Adolph Hitler".

THOMPSON: It's all politics. Don't listen to London.

JOHN: That's why I decided to announce.

COUNTESS: I thought you were planning to declare in 2004.

THOMPSON: I can't wait that long.

COUNTESS: Why not? — You'll only be ninety or so. Your father lived to be, what? — a hundred and six, didn't he?

JOHN: Mother — we may not have four more years.

COUNTESS: Why not?

(JOHN *hands his mother the Hale memo, the "Kelly Curse".*)

JOHN: They've started circulating this — but I've been expecting it.

THOMPSON: *(Pause)* What is it?

COUNTESS: *(Pause)* It says that Johnny has AIDS.

THOMPSON: *(Pause)* Let me see that. *(The old man reads; Mother and son look at each other.* THOMPSON *begins to cough and choke.)* The scum, the slime, let's get out there, I'll expose this hick ayatollah for the fascist-communist-sex pervert that he is! (THOMPSON *is frantic, trying to mobilize his wheelchair.)*

COUNTESS: It's just "politics" — remember?

THOMPSON: God, give me a drink.... *(He takes out a flask.)* He's a whoremaster and a degenerate like all the others — rounding up people, testing schoolchildren, outlawing sex — give me a drink, I said! — Thanks.... Now, let me at him. I'll make him eat this. Poor Johnnie, poor Jack — why, you're the only one of all of us who's never been—there's never been a breath of scandal—why you're as pure as a priest, for God's sake!

JOHN: *(Pause)* That's one of the problems.

THOMPSON: What? What do you mean?

COUNTESS: Here, read it: "...why Congressman Kelly has never married, and why his mother never had any more children from any of her later marriages...."

THOMPSON: Oh, the filth, the filth—wheel me out there! I'll destroy him.

JOHN: We cannot simply call the Reverend Billy Hale dirty names, Uncle Pat. We have to rise above politics, now—like the Great Depression, like World War II, like—

COUNTESS: *(Cutting under)* —Like your father—after they blew us up in the street.

JOHN: *(Pause)* What did you say?

COUNTESS: After your father and President Kennedy were killed, the country came together.

JOHN: You said "they".

COUNTESS: What?

JOHN: You said, "After they blew you up in the street."

(Pause. More band in the distance. A knock on the door.)

THOMPSON: Stay out!

KATZ: *(Off)* It's Steve Katz.—Congressman?

(Pause, then JOHN breaks the confrontation and lets STEVE slip in.)

KATZ: Mr. Mayor. Countess.

COUNTESS: Hello, Mr. Katz. You look the same. Like an old man.

KATZ: We're late. Hale's claiming victory and the network's focusing on an empty chair!

(JOHN flicks on the TV. We hear the audio.)

REVEREND HALE: *(On TV)* ...he was big, all right, Big Bill Thompson was big—a big crook—a big liar—a big bootlegger—a big sinner! And Thompson begat Thompson, and Kelly begat Kelly, and that brings us to John Thompson Kelly, Senior, the richest man in America, his father, who sat in his Kelly Towers on Lake Shore Drive and pulled strings into the White House—

(JOHN turns off the TV. The COUNTESS takes THOMPSON's flask and pours them all drinks.)

KATZ: It's war. — I don't think your mother should be exposed to it....But you have to get over there now, and call his bluff.

(The COUNTESS takes hold of THOMPSON's wheelchair.)

COUNTESS: Aged and women first. — Is it a crime in this day and age not to be married or a womanizer? To be a secular priest like my son? To be married to politics?

KATZ: But I think only the candidate can confront these kinds of —

COUNTESS: Johnny! I mean, you are not gay, are you?

JOHN: No.

COUNTESS: Of course not. And you're not infected with anything beyond terminal ambition, are you?

JOHN: My health is perfect.

COUNTESS: Of course it is. You're a "hunk". A perfect mind in a perfect body — so let's go out there and give that "whited sepulcher" the "good news".

JOHN: *(Pause)* Just a minute. — Here is what we are going to do — A — I'm going over there, B — when and if I decide you can be helpful, I'll call on you. And, I will make that judgment. *(Pause. KATZ proffers the dossier on HALE's sex life.)* I don't need that.

(JOHN leaves with KATZ. THOMPSON and the COUNTESS make a drink. She switches on the television.)

ANCHOR: *(On TV)* ...just learned that Congressman Kelly is on his way to our booth — what? — Ray Kraft?

KRAFT: *(On TV)* Rob, the word here is that Kelly's closest advisers have urged the candidate not to confront the Reverend Hale — whom they consider a loose cannon —

(Lights cross-fade to the Media Room, seen earlier.)

ANCHOR: Just a minute — he's here, the — *(JOHN and AIDES enter.)*

JOHN: Thank you....Reverend Hale — *(The two lock eyes.)* Reverend Hale — if you have anything to say about me or my family, you can say it to my face, now. Here and now... I'm waiting....

REVEREND HALE: It's not me. It's the American people who have a right to know who you really are.

JOHN: I think that the American people know exactly who I am.

REVEREND HALE: Disinformation!

JOHN: What?

REVEREND HALE: "Disinformation". The Kelly myth. — The people want the truth.

JOHN: The truth? Then why don't you tell it?

REVEREND HALE: Jesus said, "I am the truth, the way, and the—"

JOHN: *(Interrupting)* But you're not Jesus! You're a demagogue and a liar who stands on the Bible and wraps himself in the flag, who runs as a Democrat, and pretends to—

REVEREND HALE: That's right! I'm an old-fashioned Democrat, praise God.

JOHN: You're an old-fashioned liar, Sir, and your aim is to sow panic and hate and to disrupt the democratic process—

REVEREND HALE: No, oh, no, that's where you're wrong. I am bringing a message of love to this election. Love. And that's the real issue here — love and abstinence, which is what I stand for, as against lust — lust and license which is what you stand for!

JOHN: I stand for the truth!

REVEREND HALE: "O, ye generation of vipers!" Are you willing to take a blood test? I am!

JOHN: No — it's time for the facts now. — This so-called newspaper speaks for itself. The Reverend Hale and his hate merchants have printed and distributed one of the most shocking documents I have ever seen. Let me sum it up for those who haven't seen it yet — I understand that so far it's only here in Chicago that it's been distributed.... All right — it's entitled "The Kelly Curse". *(He holds up the* Family Enquirer.*)* And inside is a diagram, a so-called "family tree". See, here.... My father's mother's father, Mayor William Thompson of Chicago, and his son, my grandmother's brother, my uncle, Mayor Patrick Thompson of Chicago. And Pat Thompson, though not well, is here today to speak to you, and he will, and so will my mother, who's just flown in—

REVEREND HALE: America loves your mother!

JOHN: She will be here.... Now, here, we have my father's father, Mayor Michael Kelly of Chicago, for whom this building is named. The names Kelly and Thompson are on the thruways, and the hospitals, and the bridges, and the shelters because these men gave to this city and it citizens — they gave and they built.

REVEREND HALE: They "gave" their name — and they took the rest!

JOHN: I will tell you what they took, if you will let me finish.

REVEREND HALE: Start with the money! Are you willing to take a lie-detector test?!

JOHN: Will you let me finish?

REVEREND HALE: Start with the bootlegging. Did Big Bill Thompson shake hands with "Public Enemy Number One", John Dillinger, or not?

JOHN: May I finish?

REVEREND HALE: Didn't Big Bill and your Uncle Pat go to John Dillinger's funeral?!

JOHN: ...Yes, they did, they did go to John Dillinger's funeral.... And so did seventy-five thousand other people go to that funeral in an abandoned Illinois corn field — and do you know why? — Because in 1932, desperate out-of-work Americans got it into their heads that the gangster Dillinger was some kind of Robin Hood.

REVEREND HALE: We don't need any communist history lessons, we—

JOHN: No, you need an American history lesson, because what—

REVEREND HALE: And your family made crime legal, they worked with the bootleggers and the—

JOHN: Bootleggers, yes, and "Reds", you were going to say, yes, and the "Wobblies", and the Knights of Columbus, and went to—

REVEREND HALE: You heard it! You heard it! He's soft on crime, soft on corruption, soft on communism, and he tries to—

JOHN: And hard on hypocrites! You're leading a lynch mob down— (JOHN *brings out the "Curse" leaflet.* HALE *whips out his own copy.*)

REVEREND HALE: —Hide the fact that you are, yourself, a carrier of the disease! Passed down to you from your famous father. That you are a carrier of disease and corruption — the Hellspawn: the last and sterile male member of a damned and corrupt line of power brokers and corporate raiders who betrayed the country that gave them everything—

JOHN: What disease? Stop right there!

(HALE *becomes a fearsome prophet.*)

REVEREND HALE: "Go to now, ye rich men, weep and howl for your miseries that shall come upon you."

JOHN: You are a "false prophet", Hale!

REVEREND HALE: "...Eyes full of adultery, and that cannot cease from sin." — I'm going to name your name, now, because the "day of the Lord is coming like a thief in the night", Kelly!

JOHN: You're a prophet of hate, Hale, and "Whosoever hateth his brother is a murderer"!

REVEREND HALE: The "devil" can quote scripture!

JOHN: Are you trying to start a riot, Hale?

REVEREND HALE: "Sodom and Gomorrah...fornication and strange flesh" — that's your story, Kelly!

JOHN: Stop!

REVEREND HALE: "The sins of the fathers" — I accuse you of the sins of your father!

(He throws more leaflets.)

JOHN: Stop! — Stop there. Before the cameras and the American people, I demand that, in the name of decency, you produce a single shred of proof that my father or I suffered from a sexually communicated disease. Prove it! Prove it, now, or have the honesty to get down on your knees — something you do every week on your "Electronic Church" when you beg for funds — get down on your knees, now, here, and ask God and the people of the United States to forgive you for your mad and reckless lies!

(At that moment, the COUNTESS, PAT THOMPSON in his wheelchair, and entourage enter the booth. Sudden silence.)

REVEREND HALE: There! There is the proof. — Ask her. Ask your mother. She knows! — Poor woman — she knows....

(JOHN lunges toward HALE, but is held almost in mid-air by his own guards, but HALE is injured.)

JOHN: Creeeeep!

REVEREND HALE: Ask her what your father did to her — infected her — and through her, you — and through you and your generation, all America!

(HALE exits through the parted crowd, in the hush. JOHN turns to face his mother. Pause. The COUNTESS turns and exits. Her son follows her. The old man, THOMPSON, wheels forward to the camera.)

THOMPSON: Hale, come back here — you phony! — Now listen, you people out there, you know me. I'm a politician, yes, but I've never lied to you, I've always —

HALE'S CHRISTIAN MAJORITY: *(Off)* "Onward Christian Soldiers...."

(THOMPSON gesticulates, his lips move, the singing drowns the scene; he strains in vain as the lights cross-fade to the candidates' room.)

(In the candidate's room, the COUNTESS *stalks in, followed by her son, who slams the door on his entourage. They turn on and attend to the television. The news program is the one going on in the Media Room.)*

ANCHOR: Jeff—the Countess de Toledano, the former "Queen of Chicago", as she was called, Virginia Kelly, the mother of John Kelly the Second. This is a woman idolized by the American people for her courage after her husband's murder, as well as her wit and style, her great—

SECOND ANCHOR: She is easily one of the most famous women in the world, a legend who flew here to be with her son when he announced his candidacy for the presidency, and then to have this happen: Her son, Congressman John Kelly, violently attacked an older man. Let's run a clip of that confrontation again.

(Lights down in Media Room. Sound of HALE's *challenge, "Ask her..." etc., ring out, on the set in the Candidate's Room. The* COUNTESS *whirls from the bar.)*

COUNTESS: Turn it off, Johnny!

(He turns off the set. Silence and sounds from the distance. The COUNTESS *hands* JOHN *an aspirin container to twist open. He does, then she takes two and lies down in a reclining chair. Still stunned,* JOHN *leans against a wall. His voice is low and choked.)*

JOHN: Why did you do that? Why didn't you wait until I called on you to meet the press?—Why did you come in like that and cut me off, when I was about to expose that— *(She cuts in, her voice low and melodic, her eyes closed.)*

COUNTESS: —Please put some ice in this. And turn off one of those spotlights.

JOHN: You destroyed my confron—

COUNTESS: I saved your ass, Johnny!—You could have killed him.—I'll get it myself.

(She rises, gets ice, paces, her voice leashed, but stinging. She turns off one bank of lights.)

JOHN: You are outrageous. Sit down and listen. We have to get out in front of this. You do understand that, don't you, Mother?

COUNTESS: "Get out in front"? You mean....

JOHN: Put it behind us!

COUNTESS: "Behind us"? You mean as in "Satan, get thee behind me"?

JOHN: Sit down!

COUNTESS: No! *(Pause, then, suddenly, she embraces her son.)* Ahh, Johnny, Johnny.... Drink some of this. Go on.... They're scum, Son, all of them.... Why give them the satisfaction....

JOHN: Mother, it's on the tube, it's on the wires.

COUNTESS: In the "air".

JOHN: Yes.

COUNTESS: Well...it's only character assassination.

JOHN: What do you mean?

COUNTESS: There are worse things.

JOHN: No, there aren't.

COUNTESS: Oh, yes there are. *(Pause)* And there are also worse things than not being president.

JOHN: You don't understand.

COUNTESS: I don't? — I've seen four generations of corporate and political animals in my time. Now, while it's true that my side of the family is one weary unbroken chain of cops, clerks, and courthouse "old boys" reaching back to George II, and the old Bay Colony — and they only went to prison roughly every other generation, leaving their spawn to slug their way back up Mars Hill to the top of the heap again, just in time to kick the rascals out who had, during the previous stink and scandal, in their turn, jailed our fine old family. I should say, "mine", not "ours", because, of course, your father's people stretching back to the Ur-Kellys and aboriginal Thompsons didn't so much "break" the laws as they did "make" them — so that by the time my grandpa Charlie Chastain had made his money and could afford to finance not only elections, but my meteoric career as the "All-American Sub-Deb of the Year" — as *Time* magazine liked to put it — your father actually stood to gain by, ah "grafting" on to my "born-again", ah, "stock".... So I do, I do understand what we laughingly call "politics".

(Pause; the bells sound in the distance.)

JOHN: Mother, you've lived abroad for twenty-five years. This is not the same country you left in 1975.

COUNTESS: No?

JOHN: Not at all. The "American Century", as you people used to call it, is gone.

COUNTESS: "Gone with the wind".... Yes.... We're afraid of you, Europe's afraid of you — the whole world — "Watch out, America's got rabies!" — Not Russia, not the United Arab Republic — you, we're afraid of you.

JOHN: Not of me.

COUNTESS: No, of course not, you're John Kelly the Second. Everybody but you.... That's why I came over.

JOHN: Why?

COUNTESS: To help you become the president of the United States. So that you could try to save it all.

JOHN: *(Pause)* Except that you don't really think I can.

COUNTESS: No, if anyone can, you can. If you can control that temper. You were frightening.

(Pause. A pounding at the door and the voice of STEVEN KATZ.*)*

KATZ: *(Off)* John? — John, we have to talk.

JOHN: Not now, Steve. I'm in the middle of something.

KATZ: *(Off)* It's critical, John. — We're losing control of the event. It's getting away from us.

JOHN: I'm sorry, Steve, I need some time to work out a —

KATZ: *(Off)* Jack — at least turn on the TV, then do what you want.

(Pause. JOHN *turns on the set. Lights cross-fade to the Media Room, left. The* ANCHOR *and* CONSTANCE CONRAD *are breaking a story.* CONSTANCE CONRAD, *63, is a "former show girl". Now, she is purposefully plain. Drawn and ill, she speaks in rapid, jagged bursts.)*

ANCHOR: ...And your stage name was Constance Conrad. Now, this document alleges that you met John Kelly, Senior, in 1959 in, ah, let's see....

CONSTANCE: ...in Las Vegas. I was in the line and a friend of Senator McCurran had arranged for me to meet Hank Martello, who was headlining at Nero's — this was 1959 — so, then, Hank introduces me to John Kelly, this was before, so, then —

ANCHOR: If I can just cut in. This was 1959. Now, in 1960 Mr. Kelly was John Kennedy's campaign and finance chairman. How did you continue to —

CONSTANCE: —From '59 on— Vegas, Palm Springs at Bing Crosby's place, New York in Spyrous, uh, somebody's office, then, of course in Palm Beach, and Berlin, when we —

ANCHOR: Berlin? — Excuse me, we're talking about your love affair with the —

CONSTANCE: John Kelly, Senior — Jack and I. That is correct. Until, uh, his death.

ANCHOR: You were Constance Conrad, then.... Now, you're Mrs. Peter Arabedian—

CONSTANCE: I was the "former" Constance Conrad, my original name was Betty Bowater, my father was from Sheffield, England.

ANCHOR: Your affair with John Kelly has been corroborated, based on FBI files released to World Cable Network under the Freedom of Information Act, so my question to you is why you have chosen now to make a public statement.

CONSTANCE: I'm dying.

ANCHOR: You—you say that you're—

CONSTANCE: —Dying. I am.

ANCHOR: Is it true, Mrs. Arabedian, that you are a follower of the Reverend Billy Hale, and that he has—?

CONSTANCE: I'm a follower of my Lord and Savior, Jesus Christ, but, yes, I'm one of Reverend Hale's flock. In fact, I live and work at Familyland in the "Mothers for Jesus" clinic.

ANCHOR: And did he—

CONSTANCE: And I confessed myself to him whenever I first got real sick, two years ago, and he took me to a lawyer—Mr. Milton Marks, Esquire—so that I could get justice—

ANCHOR: Now, let me be clear. You are announcing, today, a law suit, a legal action against the family of the late John Kelly, claiming that sometime between the years 1959 and—

CONSTANCE: Up until the day he died. Yes, Sir. And I never ever again had a sexual relationship from that day to this, and that's how I—

ANCHOR: But, just a minute, Mrs., uh, you claim now, according to this legal action, that you're dying of a quote "AIDS-related infection...." that, ah, you—

CONSTANCE: —Caught from him, probably right here in Chicago, up in Kelly Towers, between the years of—

ANCHOR: I know, but AIDS didn't exist in 1960 or 1961, it—

CONSTANCE: Only Jesus knows that—but I believe it did, too, and he had it! He told me that he'd had women all over the world—

ANCHOR: That is your allegation. But you remarried, you married, so who do you claim that—

CONSTANCE: I married Peter Arabedian on his deathbed at Familyland. —He never regained consciousness. —The Reverend Hale conducted the service.

ANCHOR: You mean....

CONSTANCE: He's with Jesus today. The Reverend Hale conducted the service.... I loved John Kelly. Ran around Vegas before I met him, but, after, there was never anyone else for me—till Jesus came into my life as my personal savior.

ANCHOR: And when was that?

CONSTANCE: December 11, 1963, the day he died, and I found my redeemer.

ANCHOR: *(Pause)* And the late Mr., uh, Arabedian, he—

CONSTANCE: —He never so much as laid a finger on me. It was a marriage in Christ, Reverend Hale officiating, for Familyland.

ANCHOR: But why a law suit, now, against the Kelly family?

CONSTANCE: Because he gave me AIDS—he didn't mean it—

ANCHOR: You mean John Kelly—

CONSTANCE: But after he died, I contacted his wife, and his uncle, and they wouldn't even meet me, because I was pregnant with his child, and I needed advice, and I was sick, then, and—

ANCHOR: You were pregnant?!—That's not in your legal action.—I want to inform our affiliated stations that we're going to continue on with our coverage of this breaking story.—Now, will you say that again, please?

CONSTANCE: Yes, Sir, this is the first time I've ever told this in public.

ANCHOR: What happened to—

CONSTANCE: I had an abortion—I sinned, but Jesus—

ANCHOR: This is astonishing.—Again, I'm going to ask our affiliates to stand by, because we're going to go over our time—

(Lights cross-fade to the candidate's room, right. JOHN and the COUNTESS stand in front of the TV; JOHN turns it off. Possible act break, here.)

(Continuous action; pause.)

JOHN: Did you ever know her?

COUNTESS: No.

JOHN: Know about her?

COUNTESS: No.

JOHN: The old stories.... God, it's so sickening.

COUNTESS: Lies. In my day, the scandal sheets were somehow more, ah, innocent.

JOHN: All lies?

COUNTESS: The man was the king of the corporate world. There have been at least a half-a-dozen books and articles about or by so-called "former mistresses." Think about it. The man worked eighteen hours a day under total scrutiny.

JOHN: *(Pause)* Lies or exaggerations?

COUNTESS: Both.

JOHN: What does that mean?

(A knock and STEVE KATZ's *voice.)*

KATZ: *(Off)* Jack, are you listening to it?

JOHN: *(Shouts)* No!

KATZ: *(Off)* Jack, you've got to let your Uncle Pat in. He can help us.... Jack, Mayor Thompson is here, you've got to let —

*(*JOHN *unlocks the heavy door.* STEVE KATZ *wheels* THOMPSON *in. The* MEDIA *boil into the doorway. The door is fought shut.)*

THOMPSON: Give me a drink, for God's sake.... Ahh, my God....
(To the COUNTESS*)* How are you, Gin?

COUNTESS: *(As if reading)* "The candidate's mother looked becoming in her widow's weeds by Carlo of Seville...." — Have another drink, Pat, then let's get out of here.

THOMPSON: I will. Son, we're in trouble. — Leave me alone, Katz.

JOHN: No, we're not. This is a test, the test that can make me unbeatable.

KATZ: Excuse me, Jack, but you're not aware of what's going over the television news, while we're —

JOHN: I'm aware.

KATZ: You saw it?

JOHN: Enough. I heard enough.

KATZ: Well, that woman's been around for years, but this is different — A, she's dying of AIDS, B, she's working with the "Family Majority", and C, she never before said anything about a kid —

JOHN: Does she have AIDS?

KATZ: She took a test. She's got —

THOMPSON: —She's got a kid out there, somewhere, that could be your half-brother.

(All talk at once, until THOMPSON *shouts them down.)*

KATZ: No, no, Mayor, that's not what she said—

COUNTESS: Pat, you're drunk or senile, or both. Let's get you home—

JOHN: What? What do you mean? Let him talk—

THOMPSON: *(Interrupts)*—Goddammit, I know what she said. But how do you know it's true?! *(Pause)* She said she had an abortion. But that's not what she said when I met her in 1960.... She said, then, that she had had a son by, ah, your father, Jack, and she wanted to show it to me to prove that she wasn't a—and she did. She took me out to Deerfield, Wisconsin and showed me a baby.... Fix me a real drink, will you, Katz?

(Pause. The COUNTESS *and* JOHN *both try to talk over the old man:)*

(Together:)

COUNTESS: What are you saying, Pat? Are you mad? You mean to say that this mad woman talked to you—when?—in 1960?

JOHN: Mother, is this the first time—Mother, will you please answer me. Mother, Uncle Pat!

THOMPSON: What?

JOHN: *(Pause)* This is crucial. Don't drink that. Just a moment, please. You believe that this woman—

KATZ: Constance, uh—

THOMPSON: Conrad. Constance Conrad. I knew her. Period. She showed me a baby boy. Period...and no, I do not know whose it was, and no, I did not believe her.—Katz, you got eyes like a pay-toilet, don't look at me like that....

COUNTESS: *(Pause)* What did you do? *(To* JOHN*)* He's mad and drunk.—Pat, she just said on television that she never met me or you.

JOHN: Take it easy, Uncle Pat.

THOMPSON: Get out of here, Katz.

JOHN: Steve is my chief adviser, he's—

THOMPSON: Get him out of here.—Don't you see—it doesn't matter what the truth was—or is—all Hale has to do, now, is produce a forty-year-old white male Caucasian and that's it—it's all over. And Mr. Katz knows it, so it's better if he's not here for this discussion because, then, when it leaks he can't be blamed, because it is crucial, because your father lived and died the way he did, and because your mother is still alive—and, finally, because this Conrad woman can destroy us all—and you don't want to know about that.

(Pause. STEVE freshens THOMPSON's drink, then exits.)

JOHN: Uncle Pat—Uncle Pat? I think it's time for you to go home, now.

THOMPSON: Don't talk to me like I'm a vegetable, Johnny Boy. Tell him, Gin, tell him.

COUNTESS: Tell him what, Pat?

THOMPSON: That it's time to get out.

(The COUNTESS tucks the old man in, and wheels him to the door.)

COUNTESS: Now, Pat, it's time we all went home. No, now, don't get cross.

(She sings a bit of "Londonderry Air" to him and he joins in softly. Pause.)

THOMPSON: God bless you, Gin.... Yes, it's time to go home now—all of us.—Listen, Jack, when I met with her, that woman—shhh! let me say it and then I'll leave you alone—in, uh, 1959, I told her that if she ever repeated that story I'd make sure she went straight into an asylum. Here's the deal, I told her. I'll give you a sum of money, and take the child to a Catholic adoption service, no questions asked.—How much do you want? I asked her.—Nothing, she said, not a dime....She'll say anything, Jack—get out of it now before she can change her story again—about the child. *(To the COUNTESS)* Tell him to get out, Gin. Her saying she never met me means she's waiting to hit us with it blindside.—That's why I changed my mind. This is not our year. I'm sorry, Son.

JOHN: Mother?

COUNTESS: Shhh, Pat. Here's one for the road.

THOMPSON: Ya don't believe me, do you?

COUNTESS: Shhh. You have a part of the truth, Pat, you always do—but are you sure?—There were so many, ah, young women around in those days—film stars and girls from—

THOMPSON: Sure—"stars of the evening", they call them in the old country.

(He hums the tune.)

COUNTESS: And I think that you could have confused an incident involving your brother Michael when he was mayor. *(To JOHN)* Your grandfather, or Big Bill, before him—

THOMPSON: I'm confusing nothing. I never even talked to Jack about it because you had just come out of the hospital and he was worried—remember?...about that and about...anyway, it was that time—not Michael or Big Bill, or the time the maid claimed I asked her to horsewhip me, up on the peninsula in '37.... *(He laughs and coughs.)* Sex! Sex and politics, Johnnie Boy, that's the music of power — pumping-pumping-pumping — the old song and dance. *(Laughing and coughing)*

COUNTESS: Pat, Pat, you've tired yourself. Come on, now —

THOMPSON: But not you, boy, no, you're clean — you're the clean Kelly. Clean, clean, clean....

(JOHN *opens the door and calls* AIDES *to help take the old man out. He sings, with him, another verse of "Danny Boy". Then, as the song winds down, the old man seems almost asleep.)*

THOMPSON: ...Not our year....

JOHN: *(Soothing)* Not to worry, Uncle Pat, we'll throw the rascals out.... "Time for a change."

THOMPSON: Come here, Son, I'll tell you a bedtime story. I been listenin' to calls for change since before your father was born — and I sez to him, "Jack," I sez, "stay away from politics because the only thing all those great reformers and 'men of the people' ever changed was their underwear." Hah! Forget about reform, Boy, Chicago ain't ready for it. *(Laughing)*

COUNTESS: That's enough, now, Pat, go home to bed.

THOMPSON: Katz, you grew up in New York, tell him the score. — Hey, Katz, c'mon: "Tammany, Tammany...."

(KATZ *joins* PAT *in the old vaudeville song. Then, the* COUNTESS *chimes in as they start to wheel* PAT *out.)*

ALL: "Stick together at the polls, you'll have long green wam-pum rolls/ Tammany, Tammany.... Swampum, swampum, get the wam-pum — Tam-ma-ny!"

(AIDES *wheel* PAT *out.* JOHN *is alone with the* COUNTESS.)

JOHN: *(Pause)* That crazy story.

COUNTESS: Oh, he's certifiable. He has been for years, but that's what made him the family prophet — one of the greatest politicians of his time, and, perhaps, your father's shrewdest teacher. All the precincts and the wards of metropolis twist through his mind in all their crazy angles. Poor old Pat, he's told so many lies that he can't distinguish memory from myth anymore. — Like the rest of us.

JOHN: Except me. I remember everything.

COUNTESS: *(Ignoring* JOHN*)* No, but that's the point. Because they're a little mad, all the really gifted politicians understand that "lonely crowd" out there.

JOHN: Poor Uncle Pat — you've all forgotten who you are.

COUNTESS: I've been around them for so long—the "movers and shakers"—that I have an inkling of how they think, and read the public's mind and vice versa.... He may be old and crazed and, as always, half-potted—but that's exactly why we have to listen to him.

JOHN: Not anymore.

COUNTESS: The "Fox of the Fourteenth Ward." Vox populi. I'm afraid it's true. Some men, like your uncle, begin to tell the truth when they're very old—like others get religion, or grow breasts.

JOHN: *(Pause)* The truth?

COUNTESS: *(Pause)* If that woman decides to say that she, ah, that she had a child, then....

JOHN: Now wait. Let's not all get carried away.—No, let me make a point. First, she said that she had an abortion—not a child, an abortion. Now—wait, please, listen—even if Uncle Pat's shaggy dog story were to be true—and I say "if"—that child, that, ah, infant *(Starting to laugh)* could not have been his, my father's, because she claims—she claims that she aborted his, Father's—if you believe any of her story at all, which I do not—so that any so-called baby that Uncle Pat claims he saw in some drunken haze in 1959 or '60—he can't even remember which—couldn't have been his, my father's, but had to be someone else's....

(They laugh mirthlessly, then sit.)

COUNTESS: What do you want to ask me?

JOHN: What?

COUNTESS: Don't you want to ask me anything?

JOHN: We don't have much time now....Well...I've read about the, uh, miscarriages.

COUNTESS: Yes.

JOHN: Were there two or three?

COUNTESS: Three—I believe.

JOHN: Don't you know?

COUNTESS: Memory goes. Look at poor Pat.

JOHN: I know, but something as important as the loss of a—

COUNTESS: There is nothing more unimportant in the world than a miscarriage—in objective terms—or, for that matter, an abortion.—Don't look at me like that.

JOHN: *(Pause)* You play that role—"La Conquistadora".... I do want to ask you one thing.

COUNTESS: Ask. Then I'll go back to my castle in Spain, and you will...what?

JOHN: Become the next president of the United States. Tell the truth. Set the record straight.

COUNTESS: "Perception". Caesar's wife. *(Sings)* "I saw a man. He danced with his wife/ in Chicago...."

JOHN: Perception. It's important. It's political reality.

COUNTESS: You do see that?

JOHN: I do.

COUNTESS: Do you?

JOHN: Well, if my record as "Honest John Kelly" who's never been touched by a scandal means anything, it means that I know about the "appearance" as well as the fact.

COUNTESS: Do you have a private life, Johnny?

JOHN: I have a "public life". Period. And I'm asking the questions, Mother. — Did you ever, years ago, hear anything about this woman?

COUNTESS: No, I don't believe so.

JOHN: Or any other? Try to remember.

COUNTESS: No.

JOHN: You're positive. That, you would remember. — True?

COUNTESS: I've told you already — the past doesn't exist....Loss is irrelevant — "I forget — therefore I exist."

JOHN: *(Pause)* You know — you're a very difficult woman.

COUNTESS: That's what they all say. *(She stands, touches his hair. Picks up her coat.)* Get out, Son. It could be true. Anything could be true.

JOHN: Explain.

COUNTESS: You don't know where it will all end. Uncle Pat in his geriatric delirium has a vision of some homeless tramp turning up claiming that he's the natural son of John T. Kelly — although why even that should, as they say, "impact" on you, I do not know. But the point is, it could happen — the cities are roaming with madmen. And, more, it stirs some dim and not quite forgotten revenant, an old ghost, with white hair like your Uncle Pat, who whispers in their ear, "A jealous husband did it."

JOHN: What do you mean a "jealous husband"?

COUNTESS: What? — Yes, or, sometimes, a "jealous lover". There was even one operatic variant that I, I was the target of the assassination.

JOHN: I never heard that.

COUNTESS: Oh, yes, people will say anything. They will say that your father bought the presidency for John Kennedy with the bootleg millions of the Kelly clan and the Thompson machine. And that, then, the two fair-haired boys—Kelly and Kennedy—went on a power binge and got what they deserved. Stupid with fame and glory, they would be stationary targets—caught forever, between the cross-hairs, frozen in the amber of fame.... But the best story of all is that your father was maimed but not killed and that he has been alive all these years—but a vegetable—alive in Spain, hidden—you guessed it—in the depths of the Count de Toledano's estate under my loyal and loving control!... People will say anything—and you have to be ready.

JOHN: *(Pause)* I am ready. You trained me—groomed me like an animal. So I'm ready.

COUNTESS: Are you? You think that if you win you can lay to rest decades of bad history and lies?

JOHN: I can.

COUNTESS: Well, I can't.—So, I'm going to crawl away again.

JOHN: The media won't dare to ask you about a pack of ancient lies and a—

COUNTESS: No, but behind the old lies are the old facts.

JOHN: The what?

COUNTESS: The old facts.

JOHN: And they are...?

COUNTESS: Banal. The small sins of a great man.

JOHN: You mean Big Bill and Uncle Pat and all the—

COUNTESS: No—I'm talking about your father: Your father was America and America was him.... And you were his child, lucky Johnny, the child of luck, and, now, they're coming after you, and I don't intend to stay here and watch.

JOHN: You can't leave now. (JOHN *walks over to block her way by standing in front of the door. A bell chimes the hour in the distance.)* ...What do you mean the "small sins of a great man"?—What "old" facts? What are you afraid of?

COUNTESS: *(Pause)* You. Afraid for you. They can't touch me, now. But they can touch you with this "sexpionage".

JOHN: Stop there! That's the second time you've used the word "they".—They killed him, you said. They murder. Who are they?

COUNTESS: They know who they are!

JOHN: What-do-you-know?

COUNTESS: Nothing. — Because I was stupid with fame, too, then. I still am. But I can add one and one. — Can you?

JOHN: One and one is two.

COUNTESS: No. One plus one is still one.

JOHN: You're full of riddles, Mother.

(A voice at the door)

VOICE: We have some food, here, Congressman, if you—

COUNTESS: Yes.

JOHN: No.

COUNTESS: —Listen, everybody knows that the Kelly men were world-class cocksmen. So, now, the media reaches down into the bowels of its freeze-dried computer files and comes up with a representative sample of starlets and groupies — and they ask me if I knew my husband was entertaining Candy or Sandy or Randy or all of them on the fiftieth floor of the Kelly Towers?

JOHN: Were you faithful, Mother?

COUNTESS: I was loyal, Son — and I had the pretty choice of making fine and pitiful distinctions such as — "Oh, no, not all of them — not all of them at once" — or playing to the gallery for tears — "How could I, I was in seclusion that spring and summer, trying not to have another miscarriage!"

(The COUNTESS' harsh laughter turns to outraged and choked grief. Her son holds her.)

JOHN: Mother, I'm not trying to hurt you — but I have to know.

COUNTESS: Let me go. Let me go home.

JOHN: You are home. They can't hurt you any more than they have. — Now, I'm saying "they".

COUNTESS: *(Laughing, again, then winding down into depression)* ...Retailing that horse-shit — dining out on your father and Jack Kennedy and Elvis Presley — all alive and well somewhere in "Gringotenango", impregnating the Third World — forever young, forever green...or in the hands of plastic surgeons.... Ahhh, Johnnie Boy, once they eat you alive, the mob, and they will, there's no escape — you're trapped in the digestive tract of history, forever — with no one but Elvis and Marilyn Monroe and the rest of them.... *(Whispering and pointing to the ceiling)* So, get away, now. Today. *(JOHN shakes his head — no.)* Get out before they roll the next reel of the blue movie that we call history.

JOHN: Roll it. Let's see the truth.

COUNTESS: That the casual and unremitting whoring finally reached critical mass....

JOHN: Yes.

COUNTESS: And that I finally took my revenge.

JOHN: Don't—

COUNTESS: And had him killed. I—not they—I!

(JOHN *stares, then pours both of them a drink. He tries to comfort the* COUNTESS.)

JOHN: No, that's not the truth.

(*Her voice is a lament, as she takes another drink. The phrase she sings has echoes of Marilyn Monroe.*)

COUNTESS: "...Happy birthday, Mr. Wonderful...happy birthday to you...." He was faithful, in his way—to the bitch-goddess, Fame.—Fame was his only "correspondent". Your father was a great "specimen", and he wanted a son—a John the Second—II, Junior—and a III, a third—except you aren't going to have any children, are you?—Why?

JOHN: And you tried—is that it? You had the miscarriages, and then you....

COUNTESS: We had you. And it was different. He loved me. He loved you. He loved the three of us—himself, as always, but, now, too, me, and you. We were flesh and blood. A family.... Then the pale criminal stepped out of the crowd and threw the bomb that exsanguinated and quartered my husband's beautiful body on Michigan Avenue....

JOHN: What are you hiding, Mother? Why did you say "they" —before?

(*She makes a profound effort.*)

COUNTESS: Son—there was, first, the "idea" of the assassination—then, next, the "act", itself—and, now, ever since then, there's been, there-will-always-be, the "idea of the act".—These three are not the same thing. (*Pause*) You don't know what I'm saying, do you?

JOHN: More riddles!... Did they hate him that much? Why?

COUNTESS: Why?... There was a kind of beauty in your father and his days of grace that made some people, some men, feel ugly. He stirred feelings in them that caused them to panic, so in their panic and resentment, as the Bible says, they "conspired against him...and they said, now let us see what becomes of his dream...." So, the psychopathic servomechanism who threw the bomb may or may not have been some deracinated throwaway of some brutish plot, high or low, it doesn't matter, finally—because they killed him and they killed President Kennedy and they will kill you.

JOHN: Who will? You're hiding something!

COUNTESS: Listen carefully, Son. I will say this once, and, then, silence. "Taboo".

JOHN: I have the right to know.

COUNTESS: How was your father murdered?

JOHN: —A bomb.

COUNTESS: No.—A boomerang.

(She seems lost in a dream of grief.)

JOHN: A what?

COUNTESS: The plot to kill Fidel was a boomerang. A little chicken—like you—that came home to roost.

JOHN: Mother?

COUNTESS: Castro.... All the President's men were frantic. So the President turned to his chief adviser, and fixer, your Uncle Pat. Uncle Pat called on your father for help, and your father—who loved the President—turned, in his turn, to the "Boys". *(Thumb on nose)* Boom-boom. The "Boys" from Chicago, and Miami—and so, then, they killed him....

JOHN: Killed who?

COUNTESS: Fidel Castro.

JOHN: No, they didn't. He's alive. He's still alive.

COUNTESS: Then who did they kill? They murdered someone.

JOHN: Mother—what's the matter with you?

COUNTESS: It's a nightmare. An old dream.

JOHN: Mother, exactly what do you remember?

COUNTESS: Nothing...except that everyone gets murdered.—That's why I left—then—and why I have to leave now.

JOHN: *(Pause)* Then why did you come back home to help me?

COUNTESS: I wanted to believe that there was a new Kelly "movement" building.

JOHN: There is! People everywhere out there are huddled around their TV sets waiting—for us.

COUNTESS: They're waiting for the Reverend Hale. He flickers into focus—dead on tape—and tells them to hurry and send in their souls. That mob out there is a hopeless, helpless, diseased, dying—

JOHN: Mother! They're our people! You can't send back to Central Casting for another population. — All right, we're out of luck, you're right — we ran out of luck. You can run away to Spain, but I can't. I live here — with my people!

(Their rage mounts, until they are in full voice.)

COUNTESS: You're suffering from a congenital case of the Kelly myth.

JOHN: Why, because I don't spend my life swimming naked on that son-of-a-bitch's private island, where the —

COUNTESS: The gutter-press! You read it? You ogle the telephoto shots? You call my husband, who rescued me from that melting pot out there, you call Ruben a son-of-a-bitch? You son-of-a-bitch! They shot me! They shot me with cameras. It's the same thing — they shoot the leaders with guns, and their women with cameras — it's the same thing!

JOHN: The great lady. Two years later and you're the Countess Ruben Antonio de Toledano de Granada, the fascist queen of the international —

COUNTESS: Stop! *(Pause; her voice drops)* — At President Kennedy's inaugural, the poet called America "the gift outright".

JOHN: I know, I remember —

COUNTESS: No, you don't, you were an infant...."The gift outright" — and the breath came out of his mouth, and out of Jack's, like a clean plume of smoke — "Ask not...." All those years ago... then they killed him and your father and this country went mad. And, yes, I crawled out of the limousine while it was burning — my face was as black as black Mack Peters, our chauffeur — crawled out and over the smoking shell of that limousine — wake up! I hauled ass! I'm sorry to shock you, but I never looked back, I've never been back — except to deposit you at Harvard twenty years ago — and I never intended to come back, until you came down with messianic fever — and I did, I did come home again and I intended to say, "Vote for John Kelly, Junior, vote for my son."

JOHN: That's all I wanted, all I've ever asked you for.

COUNTESS: What, my vote? Hah! I think that is all some men really want. *(Laughs)* Black as black Mack Peters! — And they used to say that Mack and I were — *(Laughs wildly)* The "gift outright".... And I know, now, that the only way I can help you is to get away and, if I can, take you with me, before some preacher or president materializes on that tube to announce that America is Jonestown and, "Y'all come on, now, and get your Kool-aid!" *(Her laughing shout is hoarse and brutal.)*

JOHN: *(Pause)* I can't go away with you, Mother. And no, you're not a fascist. Forgive me. You're worse. You're a nihilist. You're hopeless. You could have stayed. You should have stayed. You walked away. You abandoned us. You willed yourself to forget. Our peasant ancestors came here and they worked like animals and built a "city on a hill".

COUNTESS: Rhetoric! Stop making speeches at me. Can't you just talk? *(Pause)* You look like Mr. Right, like your father's son. You even sound a little like him. But there's something missing. Something—not—there....Who are you?

(Both are hurt and in pain, trying to mask the raw contact.)

JOHN: Don't you know?... Don't you even remember me?

COUNTESS: Yes, vaguely.... Aren't you the red-white-and-blue boy—sprung from the head of Jack Kelly, the First?

JOHN: No. I'm not. I had a mother, too.—Once.

COUNTESS: You did? Oh, that's true, I remember now. Your dam was the bitch-goddess Fame.

JOHN: Yes. You.

COUNTESS: Yes. My last miscarriage. Unfinished— inside. A mutation.

JOHN: Like you?

COUNTESS: Yes.

JOHN: Empty.

COUNTESS: Dry.

JOHN: Yes.

COUNTESS: No love at all, Johnny?

JOHN: No. No love.—But something.

COUNTESS: What?

JOHN: *(Pause)* Something...the possibility, the, ah...potential to....

COUNTESS: Tell me.

JOHN: To build something.

COUNTESS: Build what?

JOHN: Something!

COUNTESS: Good-bye, Johnny. Good luck.

JOHN: Sit down. Stop running away.

(He holds her arm. A voice, off. They disregard it.)

VOICE: Do we have a statement for the late news?

COUNTESS: ...Let go.—Remember my delicate condition.

JOHN: Hah! Very delicate.

COUNTESS: Indeed. I am big with book, Sir.

JOHN: Shut-up.

COUNTESS: Big with "Big Book". So, be careful. Big Mama tells all in Big Book.

JOHN: Is it in the manuscript? Where is it? You cannot publish it without my permission. Where is it?

COUNTESS: In the womb of time.

(He shakes her again.)

JOHN: I'll rip it out of you! Where's the manuscript? What's in it? Why are you writing it? Why?

COUNTESS: For the money.

JOHN: You have nothing but money!

COUNTESS: There-is-never-enough-money. Never. — That's why I'm endorsing a new line of perfume. (JOHN *pounds the table in rage.*) — What do you think it should be called? The company wants to use "Vision", but I prefer "Power". Something like "Power". Or "Ambivalence", or "Fame". Yes, Fame!

JOHN: Tell me what you've written?

COUNTESS: Fame...that's my story. The stupidity of fame. Your father glowed with it. He came to me like a god. That crooked grin, and I fell into a dream of love and fame, until the bomb blast woke me up ten years later.

JOHN: The book.... Are you talking about the book?

COUNTESS: I'm talking about my life! — I'm to blame. I wanted and I created a great hero. I forced fame on him — and on you, God forgive me — more than anyone —

JOHN: "Forced" — on me — how?

COUNTESS: Well, now, I set you free. I give you permission to be. And you must give me permission to be.... Do you understand — I'm old, despite the plastic magic, I'm old and a little mad, and I want, with whatever time I have remaining, just to live!

JOHN: Don't publish the book. Shutup, for once! Let me have my turn. Close your mouth!

COUNTESS: I can't. The gossip and lies have to be carefully passed from generation to generation.

JOHN: Control yourself, Mother, for once. Say no!

COUNTESS: Don't worry, I won't wreck your career with the truth. I'm going to give them consolatory mythology and bull-shit chic at forty-seven-fifty a copy. — Now, kiss me good-bye.

JOHN: *(Pause)* I don't trust you.

COUNTESS: Trust? What do you know about trust — you big bundle of secrets? — It's good to trust — ah, but it's better not to.

(There is a voice at the door.)

VOICE: *(Off)* Congressman? It's Dave, Sir. World Cable News has just given us an ultimatum: If you or your mother refuse to confront this woman — the Conrad woman — right now, then they're going to rerun her interview — all night! — Mr. Katz said to tell you — he's over there now. — Congressman?

(JOHN rides over the interruption.)

JOHN: Tell me what else you're suppressing from the book!

COUNTESS: No. "Repressing"...forgetting, and forgetting that we've forgotten — I think that's what's happened to us, don't you?

(They listen to the sounds from the street. They are both as if in a fugue, spent.)

JOHN: Secrets....

COUNTESS: Secrets from ourselves.

JOHN: Tell me.

COUNTESS: Nothing.

JOHN: There is.

COUNTESS: No, you have it all, now.

JOHN: You're concealing something.

COUNTESS: There's nothing. There never was. Chicago is like Germany: Everybody knows everything and nobody knows anything. Nothing.

JOHN: You expect me to believe you?

COUNTESS: Be warned: This is the Age of AIDS, Son; don't confuse the facts with the truth; don't try to look too deep or too far into the past, or you'll go blind. Don't worry about the book: The media is like a wild beast — it lives only in the present — I'll throw them a couple of chunks of raw meat, and thirty-six hours later it'll be all over.... "Amnesia." — Should I call the perfume "Amnesia"?

JOHN: *(Pause)* I can't let you go, Mother.

COUNTESS: You have to — or kill me. *(She reaches up to kiss him good-bye.* JOHN *takes hold of both the* COUNTESS' *wrists. She screams.)*

JOHN: Talk to me, Mother, for God's sake!

COUNTESS: Johnny, you're riding for a fall! *(Her head falls on his chest.)* I'm so tired. Let me go.... Let it go. You don't need me. You have the name, let the rest go...be the new "American Man" — all future and no past — the memory slowly disappearing like wisdom teeth.... Or come away with me.

JOHN: Talk to me!

COUNTESS: To hell with the shadows following both of us — to hell with your father — *(In a slow-motion rage, JOHN forces the COUNTESS to her knees. His voice is low and dangerous.)*

JOHN: You're going to tell me.

COUNTESS: Don't marry yourself to a shadow — like I did. Forget Family Land — think of yourself, the Politics of the Flesh — "In Flesh We Trust" — live, Johnny, live, that's all!

(He kneels, even with her.)

JOHN: Like you, Mother?... You're a monster...from sub-deb to Society Queen to monster.

COUNTESS: Don't hurt me.

(He does not let her go.)

JOHN: "The gift outright".... You mortgaged our future, you put the country in "Chapter 11", and now that the continent is polluted and the population poisoned, you show up here and give me the word that politics is passé and all that matters is saving our own skin....What's happened to you? *(She struggles to free her wrists.)* You're not the mother I remember.

COUNTESS: You don't have a memory. — All you have is a pedigree and a resumé, Congressman — now, goddammit, let me go — or you'll be sorry! *(JOHN looms over his mother. Pause, then she screams.)* Katz — help!

(KATZ and entourage break in.)

COUNTESS: Johnny — I'm warning you, don't go out there. — Katz, get me out of here — get me to my machine!

(The noise, off, rises.)

JOHN: I don't need you. I never did!

(The COUNTESS is rushed out. She wheels and calls back to her son.)

COUNTESS: Stop him, Katz. Even if you have to tell him the truth: Do it, Spin-doctor!

(She exits; JOHN runs out into the street after them.)

JOHN: Mother! — Katz, come back here. Katz — Katz!

(JOHN *stands alone in the cold moonlight; a fine snow drifts down. In the distance, sounds: sirens escorting away the* COUNTESS' *limousine;* HALE's *flock singing* "Onward Christian Soldiers"; HEWITT's *troops chanting* "Are You Ready, Nigger?"; *helicopters; etc.* KATZ *reenters; sound subsides.*)

KATZ: —She's gone. C'mon, its bitter, let's get in.

JOHN: What did she mean—tell me the truth?

KATZ: Come on in. She's not herself.

JOHN: What's haunting her? What?

(*An* AIDE *runs in, calling:*)

AIDE: —Mr. Katz, Mr. Katz—Congressman—Hewitt's dead! He's dead....

JOHN: Go on.

KATZ: Where?

AIDE: Michael Reese Hospital. They say he tried to escape.

JOHN: I have to go there!

KATZ: Wait!

(*A* SECOND AIDE *runs in.*)

SECOND AIDE: The South Side's burning ! They're shooting to kill on Division Street!

(*A* THIRD AIDE *comes, shouting.*)

THIRD AIDE: The Countesses' motorcade got through!—But they're closing the airport!

KATZ: *(Pause)* Okay—all right, get everybody, get packed, we'll get a police escort and get out of here tonight!

(AIDES *scatter.* JOHN *calls after, in fury.*)

JOHN: Just a—will you get back here! *(Rounding on* KATZ*)* Who are you?! How dare you?!

KATZ: Congressman—Johnny, we have to go back to Washington. We have to regroup!

(*A helicopter hovers, announcing* "One Hour to Curfew.")

JOHN: No. Not until I know.

KATZ: "Damage Control".

JOHN: No, I'm here—and not my mother or Billy Hale or Raymond Hewitt—living or dead—is going to drive me out of this race.

KATZ: Jack, it's freezing. We have to go. — It's a disaster. Your mother was right.

JOHN: I'm at the crossroads, Steve, I can't quit now. — What did she say? *(Pointing, off, to the homeless chanting in the distance)* Listen to them.... Where do they come in? — I'm telling you that without the truth and a leader they can believe in — those poor bastards out there can't live and won't die.... What did she mean?

KATZ: We haven't got the horses! We have to wait — four more years, or eight — you're young, wait, wait.

JOHN: The truth can't wait — that's why it's the truth! And you're going to tell it, now, tonight, right here.

KATZ: I can't do it, Kid, I swore that I wouldn't, that I — until, uh, until, the, uh....

JOHN: — Until the last Kelly's dead?...But I am the last Kelly.

KATZ: No, you're still young, you're still green —

JOHN: The last. Period. And the last man left on the stage wins. That's the system, and that's the truth.

KATZ: Your mother.

JOHN: What about her?

KATZ: They'll drag her into it.

JOHN: They can't touch her. No one can. She's too rich and too thin. Tell me. Lies can't stop me — and neither can the truth. — Tell me, and then we'll go.

KATZ: *(Pause)* There's another dirty joke out there, that you haven't heard yet.

JOHN: Tell it. I've heard every dirty joke and insane story about my father that's out there. So go ahead.

(KATZ *speaks with pity, standing close to* JOHN.)

KATZ: This is not about your father.... It's about your mother.... That woman — the Conrad woman — who had the child —

JOHN: *(Laughing)* Wait. You don't believe that some pathetic street man is going to climb up out of that crowd and claim to be my illegitimate half-brother, do you? You can't believe that.

KATZ: No, I don't believe that.

JOHN: No. You couldn't believe that.

KATZ: No, I don't believe that there's anyone like that out there.

JOHN: No.... You're shaking again, you're freezing, I shouldn't have kept you out here. I'll take you in now—

KATZ: No, I'll say it and then you'll have to let me go—or kill me, too. Because I know.

(JOHN *steels himself.*)

JOHN: Krazy Katz, what do you know?

KATZ: You mother was confined to bed—they were afraid of another miscarriage. And she was wild with grief and rage. Because it got back to her that another of her husband's and Jack Kennedy's girls was pregnant, and she just couldn't take any more, so she told them, Pat and your father, that this was it, and she was leaving him and she didn't give a damn that—you don't want to hear this, Johnny—(JOHN *grips him.*) ...And they say she attacked them both, physically, and then tried to cut her wrists—ran into the bathroom—this was in the Pierre Hotel in New York, because we were traveling with the campaign, I was working on a speech and I heard it and when I ran in, they were all in the bathroom and they were begging her—they didn't know that I was listening—and they promised to get her a—Dr. Royce, James Royce, he walked out and saw me. I followed him out, he was terrified....Two weeks later they announced your birth, during the Oregon primary. Six weeks after, you were on TV during the convention.... I'm so sorry, Kid. That's all I know, but it's enough. Nobody knows for sure anymore; your uncle's not all there, and your mother, at the time, was beside herself, and, besides—now, don't look like that, Jack, besides, maybe she didn't miscarry—or abort.

JOHN: Who?!

KATZ: No, for a long time what I thought happened that day was that she found out about your father's mistress and the baby and threatened to kill her own baby—to abort or to, uh, and ran into the bathroom and that's when I came into the other room and what I heard could've referred to some double-talk they were giving her to quiet her down, because I heard her scream, "I'll call *The New York Times*! And ruin your gang-bang buddy's chance to be elected—ever!"

JOHN: *(Pause)* She wanted to kill me?... But you don't know, do you? You can't know if she miscarried!

KATZ: Not for sure, no. But what I believe is—that you're him.

JOHN: Who?—I'm who?

KATZ: Him.... The child that woman had by your father. You're the "poor bastard".

JOHN: I'm the....

KATZ: The child—that your father and your uncle took from her—that she gave them—and that they gave to your mother—all I know, for sure, is that something happened that day, and, then, something happened three years later....

(JOHN *heaves dryly, whispers.*)

JOHN: You people—were traitors.

KATZ: We were afraid. Don't judge us. We were afraid of the shadow of our own bomb.... But I believed, I prayed that it was time, now, to go forward, and so did your mother, and I think your uncle, too, though you can't ever be sure with him—we all did.... But here it is the first day of the g'damn campaign and they're starting to come out of the woodwork. The skeletons were waiting at the airport for your mother.—So, I was wrong.

(*The two huddle together for warmth.*)

KATZ: It's not to be, Kid.

JOHN: What happened?—I mean, what happened?— They say I sat in a rocker in my father's office in the Kelly Towers and waved to the cameras.—And there was a dog....

KATZ: You remember that, Johnny?

JOHN: No.

KATZ: I do.

JOHN: I don't.—Only what they show on television.... Inside my head is a tape of my life....

KATZ: Let's go home, Kid.

JOHN: I see my mother's face—at a window.—Was I a "love child"?

KATZ: What else do you see?

JOHN: Blue skies. A lake up in Michigan.

KATZ: Yeah.

JOHN: Is it a film? Is it real?

KATZ: Sure it is.

JOHN: No.—Other people's memories. Blue smoke and mirrors. All lies.

KATZ: Not everything, I mean not—

JOHN: Lies—big and little—gossip, rumors, dirty jokes: myths!

KATZ: Not everything, not all of us!

JOHN: Propaganda—.

KATZ: We tried, we believed.

JOHN: Other people's lies! I know. You people pretend to remember. But I know it's all lies.

KATZ: No, I'll prove it to you — do you remember your family place on Mackinac Island?

(Homeless begin to straggle in, carrying barrels and cans with flames inside. They huddle around their fires, below JOHN and KATZ. Snow, wind, distant sirens. JOHN searches his memory. In the distance, a far-away warning siren. Below, a homeless person moans a fragment of a hymn or song.)

JOHN: I see a big green boathouse.

KATZ: That's it. Listen, you had a wonderful childhood, you had —

JOHN: I see it on film.

KATZ: What?

JOHN: Home movies — TV specials, "The Kelly Legacy". Brought to you by "Memorex".

(KATZ works out his wallet.)

KATZ: Here, look, remember Lila? My little girl — came to visit you that last summer....

JOHN: *(Studying)* No....

KATZ: You don't? — Well, of course, you went to Spain right after, but.... You remember my wife, Edie, don't you?

JOHN: Not really.

KATZ: How she adored you?... Who else? — What about when we all came to Spain for the, uh, no....

JOHN: The wedding?

KATZ: Yeah. You stood next to your mother. You had on a uniform and a little sword? You must!

JOHN: No.

KATZ: The library, when they had the naming ceremony, by that time you were about —

JOHN: No.

KATZ: Will you stop fighting me!

JOHN: I'm not.

KATZ: The airport?

JOHN: No.

KATZ: You cut the ribbon, for God's sake.

JOHN: No.

KATZ: You were five years old!

JOHN: Nothing!

KATZ: You saluted, you laughed, you were happy —

JOHN: No!

KATZ: Yes!

JOHN: All on film. Not me. On film!

KATZ: — Doesn't any of it come back to you? — How we loved you? (JOHN *slowly shakes his head.* KATZ *starts to leave.*) I'm freezing, Kid....

JOHN: The body remembers....

KATZ: Huh?

JOHN: She said, "The body remembers" — something like that.

KATZ: Your mother?

JOHN: Was she? — You don't know, do you?

KATZ: No.

JOHN: Well, it doesn't matter!... Come on, Krazy Katz, sing me the song — so I won't go nuts. *(Shouting)* God damn it, Katz, sing it!

(KATZ, *in tears, tries to sing.* JOHN *leads bitterly.*)

JOHN & KATZ: "Tammany, Tammany,
Kelly is our big chief's name,
He's a Rothschild just the same.
Tammany, Tammany,
Willie Hearst will do his worst to Tammany."

(JOHN *laughs and dances, then attacks* KATZ.)

JOHN: That's it. I'm the "New American Man" — she said. Well, I am. With the new American disease: My memory was my immune system — and now it's gone!...

KATZ: *(Whispering)* Let it go, now, before they make you the goat.

JOHN: No — I have to do something. Look at them, for Christ's sake — *(He hits his head.)* — someone has to set us free!

KATZ: Poor bastard, we've made you crazy.

JOHN: No, I'm happy—for the first time—I'm alive, because I know who I'm not, and you have to know who you're not before you can know who you are.—I'm not following in my father's footsteps anymore—they led in a circle, nowhere, and I was a clown, a clone, a Kelly clone.... And now I'm free—my mind is free, and my body, because they're one flesh, and "one and one is still one"! *(He laughs and cries to a mighty spasm.* KATZ *groans as* JOHN *grabs him in a murderous embrace.)* I know the answer to all the riddles, now! The "Idea"—the "Act"—the "Idea of the Act"!... Go home, now, Katz....

(He puts his coat around KATZ.*)*

KATZ: My God! What are you going to do?

*(*JOHN *walks him toward the exit.)*

JOHN: Go on with the act, the idea of the act.

KATZ: What act?

JOHN: *(Pause)* It's a secret.... God bless, Steve.
*(*KATZ *bows his head, unable to speak, and exits. Alone,* JOHN *looks down on the clumps of humanity around the trash can fires. Then,* JOHN *descends and moves into the shadows, in and out of the light from the dull flames. At first, his voice is low and tentative and few pay any attention to him.)*
Hello, my name is, ah.... I'm here tonight, to, ah.... Habla conmigo? ....I need your help.... No, I mean, together we can, ah.... Hello, I, ah, want to work with you to, ah, for a brighter tomorrow....
*(*JOHN *is an alien among the shadowy figures. He moves from fire to fire, in and out of the shadows. A siren in the distance, and* POLICE *patrol the periphery. One group hums a religious hymn softly. In the distance, a raucous chorus of* "Are You Ready, Nigger?"—*the* POLICE *trot off in the direction. Sounds of distant violence, then silence and the low humming, again.)*
...Uh, you don't know me but I, uh.... I don't know you but may I talk to you?... Could we talk?...
(A HOMELESS WOMAN *holds an infant in a blanket up to* JOHN, *then she slips away. Two* JESUS FREAKS *begin to babble in tongues at* JOHN'*s feet; others in the square beat the Christians into silence.)*
No, please, don't, we all.... We all need, ah.... We have to find out who we are....
(A YOUTH *comes close to* JOHN, *to whisper in his ear.* JOHN *bends low to hear, just as an* ADULT *snatches the* YOUTH *away.)*
Wait.... We're all in the same...ah....
*(*JOHN *raises his voice for the first time.)*
Do you know me?
(Silence)
Do you know who I am?
(Continuing, louder)
I know you, and you know me.... We know each other....

(The POLICE *return to the square.)*

POLICEMAN: Hey, hold it down—or I'll move you people out of here.

(JOHN *freezes. Silence and the sound of the wind rising. The* PEOPLE *try to shield themselves. The* POLICE *stamp in the cold and exit, drinking from a Thermos.)*

(Without a coat, JOHN *searches for a place at a trash can. He shivers as he speaks, his voice low and shaking.)*

JOHN: We won't make any noise.... Look at me.... I want to tell you something.... Give me your hand.... I have to tell you something.... Don't you know me?... You knew my father—you remember him?—My father! *(Silence)* Don't you remember anything?...

(JOHN *moves into the people.... Lights fading to black, flames into darkness. The wind rises.)*

THE END

IS HE STILL DEAD?

IS HE STILL DEAD?
© 1990 by Donald Freed

For Dan and Elsie O'Herlihy

IS HE STILL DEAD premiered at the Long Wharf Theater, New Haven CT, on 8 May 1990; Arvin Brown, Artistic Director, M Edgar Rosenblum, Executive Director. The cast and creative contributors were as follows:

NORA JOYCE . . . . Julie Harris
JAMES JOYCE . . . . Ronny Graham

Director . . . . Charles Nelson Reilly
Set design . . . . Marjorie Bradley Kellog
Costume design . . . . Noel Taylor
Lighting design . . . . Marc B Weiss
Music . . . . David Fox
Sound design . . . . Brent Evans

PLACE: A Hotel, Saint-Gerand-le-Puy, France

TIME: Late November, 1940

The play may be broken into two acts at page 111.

The sitting room of the Joyces' small suite in the Hotel du Commerce is at least twenty years out of style. The door upstage to the corridor is set in a cramped entryway. Left is a doorway to the bedroom and bath. Right is an improvised cooking area, including an electric ring, a dwarf ice-box, and a window. There is a small piano.

Trunks, valises, cases stand about open, and half-packed. Books and papers are stacked on surfaces. There are a gramophone and a boy's bicycle in one corner.

For music and general consultation: To Rosemarie McCaffery, with gratitude. See "The Golden Voice of John McCormack", Volume I, Dolphin Records, #DOLE7072.

(*At curtain, in darkness, can be heard a recording of John McCormack's* Londonderry Air, *and a siren in the distance.*)

(*Lights up, 10 a.m.: A cold winter light discovers* JAMES JOYCE *standing amidst the luggage, dressed to leave the suite but paused, now, held by the music.* JOYCE *is a very frail and ill 58. His ensemble is fashionable, including gloves, overcoat, hat, stick, tinted eyeglasses, tennis shoes, bow tie, and muffler.*)

(*He stands rapt, humming along with the great song. His fading eyes survey the scattered belongings of this — yet another — temporary way-station in his life-long exile.*)

(*After a minute,* NORA BARNACLE JOYCE *enters from outside.* NORA *is near* JOYCE *in age but electric with energy despite a painful arthritic condition. She is loaded down, now, with mail, packages, and food parcels, and is warmly and smartly dressed against the cold weather.*)

(JOYCE's *voice and diction are dry, cultivated, and attenuated, except when he is carried away by* NORA's *wit and passion.* NORA's *voice is strong with its original west Irish melody and emphasis.*)

NORA: My Jesus, mercy. Did ye not hear me knock? — Will ye turn that down?

(JOYCE *is immobile.*)

NORA: (*Continuing*) Jim! Are you in a trance? — Where do you think you're moochin' off to at this hour, at all? It's bitin' cold in the street.

(JOYCE *turns, looks at* NORA, *bows slightly, and takes a step toward the door.*)

NORA: (*Continuing*) Will you howl your horses? Will ye stop? — Give me your hat till I kneel on it. (*This, as calculated, catches his fancy, makes him shrug with a silent laugh.* JOYCE *seems to say a word.*)

NORA: (*Continuing*) What? Will you speak up or turn off that "great voice" of the past!

JOYCE: Who? The man's still alive.

NORA: God and his Blessed Mother, will ye put it off! I've told you that that old-fangled Irish music is going to drive me clane and dacent up the wall.

JOYCE: It's ravishing. Don't touch it.

(*He starts to sing along.*)

NORA: If it's anyone can make a person throw up their guts, it's you. You wouldn't offer to give me a hand with this if me backside was studded with diamonds.... Oh, you're the devil's father, you are. You're the "bella figura."

(NORA *turns the music off. She puts parcels away, then crosses to the bedroom to take off her coat and hat, then re-enters to find* JOYCE *staring again and singing softly to himself.*)

NORA: What?

JOYCE: What's that?

NORA: Are you awake at all? — Where do you think you're going?

JOYCE: To look for that fellow with the visas.

(NORA *begins to prepare tea in the kitchen area.*)

NORA: Where's Giorgio and Stephen, then?

JOYCE: What's that?

NORA: Jaysus comfort me in me last agony. Standing there in the "Celtic twilight" with your hat on in the house looking like Uncle Tommy.

JOYCE: Who?

NORA: Sure that fellow could hear the grass growin'. — Unlike you.... Are you deaf as well as blind, Jim? Where's your son and grandson, I asked you. Did they get the visas, then?

JOYCE: Ahh.

NORA: Well?

JOYCE: Mm. Well, they've gone to see about the man with the visas. Was that a siren I heard?

(NORA *shakes her head and laughs.*)

NORA: What have you got in your pockets?

JOYCE: What? — Oh, stones.

NORA: Stones!

JOYCE: For the dogs.

NORA: *(Laughing)* To throw at the dogs? In the name of the Father and of the Son and the Holy Ghost. — Sit down, man, and eat your porridge. — Sit down and put something in you, and I'll read you the *Irish Times,* and there's a letter or two from Paris, but, ah, I'm sad to say, nothing at all from Mrs. Weaver, as yet.

(NORA *takes off* JOYCE's *hat and coat and brings him a dressing gown, then leads him to the table to sit. The telephone jangles. As* NORA *talks,* JOYCE *plays the piano softly — to shut out her words.*)

NORA: Hello — Giorgio! Where are you? Is Stephen with you — he's where? — Watching the bicycle? Is it broke, then? — It is. — What about the visas? — You have an automobile — ah, thank God — but it's run out of gas! — Alright, I'm listenin' — go ahead —

JOYCE: *(To himself, then sings softly)* Jesus wept, and no wonder, by Christ.

NORA: No, no, no — you're obleeged to go to the American Legation — because, because HE won't accept an IRISH passport — "I'm not a hypocrite!" That's your father's line —

JOYCE: ...The former and the latter and the holocaust...

NORA: What? — Then for pit's sake carry the gasoline on the bicycle to the automobile and drive it to the Legation and beg for the visas if you have to — so we can leave this place — TONIGHT!

(JOYCE *sings softly. She hangs up.*)

NORA: *(Continuing)* Here, come on, you're as weak and poor as a rat. I'm going to tell them downstairs that you're to have no brandy at all. You were down there last night like a drunken sleeveen — here, sit down, will you? — That's right. Start on this and I'll make you some beef tea.

JOYCE: No, I couldn't.

NORA: Sure, you're full of the gas again.

JOYCE: I couldn't stomach it. — No money from Mrs. Weaver?

NORA: No. I'll make you some "goodie," for your digestion.

JOYCE: I'm not well, I told you, I can't take any milk at all.

NORA: You've the mind of a child. You'll do for yourself, with the drink, one day, and that's the holy alls of it. — Now take your tea, at least, and keep quiet.

(*She laughs as she throws away the stones from his overcoat pockets.*)

NORA: Sure, a dog is a friend to man.... Go on drink it, it'll wash you out. And eat a piece of toast.

(*Trembling,* JOYCE *sips a little tea.* NORA *steps out into the corridor.*)

NORA: I'll see if there's a telegram at the concierge about the visas.

(NORA *exits.* JOYCE *rises to look for something and falls into a large open trunk, as* NORA *re-enters. At first she cannot find him, as he is immobile again.*)

NORA: There's no word.... Jim? Devil take him—Jim? *(She discovers him; screams, then laughs with relief.)* Jesus, Mary and Joseph! Are you alive at all? Here, stand up — are you entirely polluted from the Pernod last night?

JOYCE: "Peloothered."

NORA: Oh, shut your gob, and put your feet under the table, will you, and try not to kill yourself before we leave for Zurich. — I'm worn out with you, my arthritis is that bad again.

(They both sit and recover.)

JOYCE: I need those letters.

NORA: What letters, at all?

JOYCE: From Yeats and Shaw.

NORA: You're raving.

JOYCE: To get the visas for Zurich before —

NORA: You're too weak to walk across the room, man. Umm, my leg.

JOYCE: —Before the bloody Germans find us.

NORA: *(Improvising sardonically, holding up papers as visas)* To whom it may concern at all: Please permit the world-famous writer of dirty books, Mr. James Augustus Aloysius Joyce, and his so-called bitter-half, Mrs. Nora Barnacle Joyce, to pass, and, besides, if it wouldn't be too much trouble, their son Giorgio on account of his pleasant singing voice, and his son Stephen and his bicycle. Yours sincerely, George Bernard Shakespeare the Third!

(JOYCE *covers his mouth with his hand to laugh, as he does time and again during* NORA*'s constant stream of talk. This laughter, and sometimes rage, is precisely her purpose—anything to keep* JOYCE *alert and hopeful.)*

JOYCE: ...All the same... Will I cable Harriet Weaver about the money?

NORA: Wisha—it's not famous writers they give a damn about in Switzerland, it's having twenty thousand Swiss francs in the bank in Zurich. Sure, you can dictate a cable to Miss Weaver, to me, after the meal. Now leave off gabbin' about money, will you?

JOYCE: I can walk out on the road, like Tolstoy. And you in the lead on the boy's bicycle. — Ahh, to hell with 'em all, we'll wait here for the Germans.

NORA: Here!? This place's not fit to wash a rat in. Just as soon's Giorgio and Stephen get back, then we'll see what's what. — Now, drink your tea and I'll read you the *Irish Times*.

JOYCE: I couldn't concentrate.

NORA: You won't have to, I'll start with the "Births and Marriages." *(She opens the newspaper)* "Bell — October 22, 1940, to Clara [nee Dowling] and Howard, a son [Kevin Richard] —"

JOYCE: No!

NORA: Alright — I'll read you the "Deaths", then.

JOYCE: No, the "Personals."

NORA: All in good time. Finish your toast. — Let's see.... Mm — "McTernan [Cork] September 28 [unexpectedly] Theresa [nee Guinn] — " Would that be Kendrick McTernan's wife? Or is she still dead?

JOYCE: Not at all. *(He laughs behind his hand. Her eyes glow with an old joke. As the reading ritual continues, NORA slowly provokes JOYCE to hilarity.)*

NORA: Are you sure? I'm certain she is. Mm — "...precious mother of Pauline, Hughie, Michael, Eddy, John, Fergal, Dolores, Diarmiud, Audrie, the late Malcolm, Frank, Gus, Murry [U.S.A.], and the late Joe — "

JOYCE: "Rest in peace."

NORA: "...the late Joe... Lying in repose... Removal tomorrow... Funeral afterwards — "

JOYCE: "Belfast papers please copy."

(JOYCE finishes his tea, the energy level is moving up, now, with the building, if slightly morbid, humor.)

NORA: Ah-ha..."Anxious? Depressed? Suicidal? Phone, write, or visit the HOLY ADVISERS — "

JOYCE: Do they give the telephone number?

NORA: Wait — "Lost from Sandycove, 2 grey kittens, with peach markings — child heartbroken."

JOYCE: Help! *(He yelps with pained laughter.)*

NORA: *(Continuing)* Ah, you're a terrible fella. — "Tourist French for Adults — " *(Laughter)* "Almost any man knows how to earn money, but not one in a million knows how to spend it. — Henry David Thoreau."

JOYCE: I'm your man!

NORA: "The Seven Seas Cure — for Gentle, Natural Relief — Restful Nights, Nerves, Catarrh, Rheumatic Pain, Laxative — " *(Laughter shaking them)* What is it?

JOYCE: Seaweed!

NORA: "Authors — Your book published. Pyramid Press, One Garden Place — send cash."

(They are weeping helplessly with laughter. JOYCE *staggers about until* NORA *helps him to lie down on the sofa. At length:)*

NORA: Now, that's enough now. Give over, Jim — ah, ha... I'll read you the Flann O'Brien later.

JOYCE: Ireland — IRELAND!

NORA: Now, don't get started on that, now. Put your feet up, will you?

JOYCE: You'll kill me laughing.

NORA: Well, it's better than moochin' about with a face on you like the bottom of a pot.

JOYCE: Will I dictate the cable to —

NORA: Lie down, will you, and rest your stockings. Rest your eyes and let me get on with the work.

*(*NORA *leaves* JOYCE *on the sofa and starts to prepare the noon meal. In the silence,* JOYCE *seems to have dozed off.* NORA *tip-toes over and opens one of the letters. She reads with anxiety.* JOYCE *speaks very softly.)*

JOYCE: Annie Barnacle...

NORA: Are you asleep?

JOYCE: Your mother.

NORA: What about her?

JOYCE: Her "Death Notice."

NORA: What about it?

JOYCE: Where is it?

NORA: Sure, she's not been dead three weeks.

JOYCE: — That's true.

NORA: We'll be readin' it soon enough.

JOYCE: Annie Barnacle R.I.P.

NORA: Rest in peace.

*(*NORA *is shaken by a wave of grief, and* JOYCE *covers his eyes, too. Pause.)*

JOYCE: What's the time?

NORA: What's the difference?

JOYCE: The post. — What's the weather, now?

NORA: It's a very poor class of day. — What's your rush? *(Quoting her mother, at the window)* "Sure, there's more days than years."

JOYCE: I can hear her voice. — Is it coming down with snow?

NORA: *(Looking out the window)* All over Ireland....

JOYCE: I can hear her voice..."God's help is nearer than the door."

NORA: *(Pause)* Well — I'm going to eat a proper meal. I need strength! Giorgio can carry Stephen, and I'll carry you, right across the border.

(Despite NORA's resistance, JOYCE continues to recall years gone by. His voice has a lilt and a chuckle that finally draw NORA away from her "cooking.")

JOYCE: ...Your MOTHER could cook...I sat there at her kitchen table writing to you and she —

NORA: That luggage is full of old letters.

(She kicks a bag.)

JOYCE: —She served me a first-class tea. *(Imitating)* "Strong enough to trot a mouse on."

NORA: Look at this hyena of a suitcase, will you, filled with scribblin' from the year one.

JOYCE: — And talked a streak. *(A perfect imitation:)* "Put out the dog till we say the rosary, will ye?!"

NORA: I'm going to sell them to a museum.

JOYCE: Burn 'em all, then!

(JOYCE flares up, then returns to his reverie. NORA carefully packs up the papers and returns to the window and her vague meal preparation.)

JOYCE: *(Continuing)* ...Aye, she had a tongue in her head.

NORA: It drove my father out — he slept in the bakery.

JOYCE: Ha! She used to say that your father "drank up all the buns and loaves like a man."

NORA: He drank, she talked. — Take your rest now.

JOYCE: "The whiskey was nice and so was the maker
And under the counter was Barnacle the Baker."

NORA: Holies, will you stop gabbin'? — It's days at a time I can't get a word out of you about what we're going to do at all about leaving here, then comes the "morning after" and you're tellin' me what you had for tea in Galway thirty years and more ago.

JOYCE: ...Then you came along with Giorgio and we walked on the strand in Salthill, and sailed to the Aran Islands — do you mind that?

NORA: Can't you see I'm busy?

JOYCE: ...Grey light when we came back, music spreading down the street — from the Convent of Offerings, and the white veils of the nuns at the windows....

(NORA *tries to pull herself from the window and memory but is arrested in mid-motion. Church bells chime the hour: 11 o'clock.* NORA *has a cord [a flax] in her hand.*)

NORA: This flax is worn out....

JOYCE: ...And then a proper tea, and Giorgio asleep at the table — and "Sing us the 'Lass of Aughrim,'" begs I. And she would.

NORA: Oh, aye.

JOYCE: She would. *(Pause, then he sings softly:)*
"Oh, if you be the lass of Aughrim
As I suppose you not to be
Come tell me the lost token
Between you and me."

JOYCE: *(Continued)* "Go on," I'd say. — "Ahh, no," she'd say, "musha, it aits your heart away, I'll put the kettle on." — "Nay," say I, "sing for us." — And she'd laugh, with tears in her eyes, "Troth and sould, yous would wear out a saint."

(JOYCE's *memory of Galway produces the very accents of* NORA's *mother, as if he were a consummate actor — so that, in spite of her resolve to go forward and not backward,* NORA *begins to sing the verse. Smiling,* JOYCE *joins her.*)

NORA & JOYCE: "O Gregory, don't you remember
One night on the hill
When we swapped rings of each other's hands
Sorely against my will?
Mine was of beat gold
Your was but black tin."

(JOYCE *struggles to his feet and goes to* NORA. *He continues to sing as he tries to eat a bite of the goodie — bread and milk — that she has made.*)

JOYCE: "The rain falls on my yellow locks
And the dew it wets my skin;
My babe lies cold within my arms;
Lord Gregory, let me in."

(NORA *refuses to continue this last verse. She helps* JOYCE *to a chair.*)

NORA: But he didn't — so she drownded herself... Aye, "He drank, and she talked" — that's Ireland!

(JOYCE *sits,* NORA *returns to the cooking area. Pause.*)

JOYCE: Did you write to the solicitor, Concannon? To tell him that we want to see your mother's will in black and white?

NORA: *(Laughing)* It's money again, is it. Her "will"?! Ahh that's rich! — There won't be no will nor no money. Sure, all of Galway thinks you're a swank millionaire and going to send THEM a spot of cash. "Faith, didn't he write that dirty book and make a fortune?!"

JOYCE: She would have wanted me to have a bit of money. That I know.

NORA: That you know?! Hah!

JOYCE: Yes — howl on!

NORA: Eejut! — "Wanted YOU to have a bit of money" — wouldn't it drag the guts out of a person, to hear you.

JOYCE: I know what I know.

NORA: — Anymore than your father had so much as a broken cup to leave us.

JOYCE: That's a lie. He left me hundreds.

NORA: Yes, hundreds, an' didn' he take thousands and thousands from us?!

(JOYCE's *posturing cannot hide his remorse.*)

JOYCE: My father left me a waistcoat, a tenor voice, an extravagantly affectionate disposition —

NORA: Hah! —

JOYCE: — out of which the greater part of any talent that I may have springs and a —

NORA: — the great talent you have for draining the pubs of Europe dry —

JOYCE: Well, "Take him for all and all, I shall not look upon his like again!"

NORA: No.

(JOYCE *squints at a photograph.*)

JOYCE: I should have gone back to see him.

NORA: Then why didn't you — instead of moanin' and groanin' with guilt for the last ten years?

JOYCE: I couldn't.

NORA: Why not?

JOYCE: Because if I ever went back to Dublin, I wouldn't have been able to write about it.

NORA: Well, cheer up, will ye — your Da always said, "I've got more out of life than any white man."

JOYCE: He did, at least, read *Ulysses*.

NORA: And hated it: "Now, why can't Jim get a good sit in the Land Commission?"

(They laugh.)

JOYCE: No — I should have gone back, one last time. I promised him. — I lied. — I'm the father of lies.

(NORA comforts him.)

NORA: No, you're not — you're just a wee devil.... Give us a smile, can't ye...? He died —

JOYCE: This time of year —

NORA: — it was — and then, just after his great grandson Stephen was born.

JOYCE: Yes.

NORA: Yes.... *(She goes to a book, opens it.)* Here, read a wee bit out. It'll do ye good.

JOYCE: "...A child is sleeping;
An old man gone.
O, father forsaken,
Forgive your son!"

(JOYCE stares out.)

NORA: *(Pause)* ...All right.... What ghost are ye staring at now?

JOYCE: *(Pause)* Your mother — in her will — would have included a codicil in my favor. — That's my last word on the subject.

NORA: Good! Save your breath for your pooridge. — Eat this, now, you terrible man.

JOYCE: Go on out of that, now. I know what I know.

(NORA erupts.)

NORA: G'owa that yourself! Sure, didn't she live to eighty-two years of age, with no money from her drunken Irish husband. Live on nothin' at all — on the smell of an oil-rag — with no help from me — God forgive me! — much less you — and for what? So that she could leave you a "bit of money"!

(JOYCE stands and tries to put on his overcoat.)

NORA: It's leavin' are you? The great man that you are. — Sit down, and I'll tell you what she would've: "A penny looks down on a ha'penny, and a ha'penny looks down on a farthing."

(JOYCE *is lost in his overcoat between outrage and laughter.*)

NORA: *(Continuing)* Will you look at the look on you. Sit down before you fall down.

(*They wrestle with his overcoat, laughing to tears, again, and stumbling to the sofa where she falls half on top of him. They lie there, recovering. They then hum a little of* "Love's Old Sweet Song.")

NORA: ...Ahh — um, my leg — no, don't move, it'll pass.

(*Both laugh a short punctuation.*)

NORA: You were callin' out in your sleep again.

JOYCE: "Help!" *(Short laughter)*

NORA: All mixed up like an Irish stew.

JOYCE: "Avelaval....whish... Finn, again...mememormee..."

NORA: *(Pause)* Sure, I had my own dream to worry about.

JOYCE: What's that?

NORA: I've forgot now.

JOYCE: Let's have it. Confess.

NORA: Not now.

JOYCE: Tell it — or it'll drive you madder than you are.

(*Laughter. Then he hums softly.*)

NORA: You will poke.... It's a dance, I'm at, in Bowling Green Street. The girls are at one end of the hall — like we was.... The fellahs standin' down at the opposite end — like they did. (JOYCE *hums.*)

NORA: *(Continuing)* Sure, none of the men'd come over at all. (*He hums.*) And they were all naked.... In the dream... Don't the Irish have terrible white skin, though?

(JOYCE *hums;* NORA *rubs her breast.*)

NORA: *(Continuing)* Why are they so terrorized by it? *(Laughs)* Well, it's true, an Irish girl will do anything.
"I'm a naughty girl
You needn't sham
You know I am."

(*He laughs at that, but stops when* NORA *puts her hand on his thigh.*)

NORA: *(Continuing)* The poor things: Either they're curled up like a ball... (*She rises.*) ...or stickin' up like a hatrack.

JOYCE: *(Pause)* It's time for dictation. — Read me out the list.

(NORA *settles the writing material at the table, and reads:*)

NORA: Random House, Faber and Faber, Viking, Sam, Maria, Miss Weaver, of course, the Swiss Society of Authors and —

JOYCE: No — it's the clinic... "Dear so and so" — make it to the director, himself...

(*Both are lost in thoughts of their mad daughter, Lucia.*)

JOYCE: (*Continuing*) Uh, mm — "I am writing to you at this instant concerning my daughter, Lucia Joyce. You state that her condition is 'stable'. (*He pounds two sharp responses out of the piano.*) As we expect our French permis de sortie from day to day....

NORA: ...What are you talking about? Giorgio's running all over the town tryin' to get the visas TODAY!

JOYCE: There's no money!

(*He climbs up, weak but surging with feeling. The two intercut their raw fears at a furious pace.*)

NORA: Wisha, Jim, don't start on that — we'll get the money from —

JOYCE: — There's no money to pay her clinic bill, leave alone getting her transferred to French Switzerland, and we don't even —

NORA: — Jaysus, will you dry up for once and use your "world-famous" brain to put two and two to —

JOYCE: — And they want to call her mad because she believes she's being left to —

NORA: — Try not to go off your own head —

JOYCE: — Monsters coming to destroy her, and it's true! There are, they're —

NORA: — Have you gone mad yourself?

JOYCE: — How can I leave her there — What if they put her out before we can send for her — My God, it's tearing me in half —

NORA: You? Can't you think of someone, for once, besides yourself?!

JOYCE: The Germans — the Germans are coming, you foolish woman —

NORA: Your daughter! — Can't you think of your daughter — and what's best for her?

JOYCE: You hate her because she's an artist — like me. Let's have the truth at last!

(JOYCE *is doubled over, gasping from the ordeal.* NORA *stalks in and out of the bedroom, dressing to go out, muttering to herself in wild agitation*).

NORA: *(Stunned, then walking)* That's the last straw. The Pernod's rotted his brain. He's gone too far, now. He's burned his bridges, now. I hate you— that's the holy truth of it: with yer "clinic," and yer "maison de sante," and yer "maison de repos" — in the name of Christ, man, when will ye face it and use the hard word: Our daughter is not an "artist" she's a poor thirty-two-year-old lunatic in a lunatic asylum!

JOYCE: Help!

NORA: Didn't she try to murder me —

JOYCE: Don't you blame me —

NORA: My own child —

JOYCE: I visited her — you never did!

NORA: Picked up the chair —

(He pounds out a tune on the piano.)

NORA: — with the strength of ten — *(Picking up a chair, slowly, as if in a nightmare)* Picked up the chair and threw it-at-my-head!

(NORA's strangled cry cuts through the piano sound. Then, a long silence, and she turns to leave. JOYCE *stumbles about, pushing over luggage.)*

JOYCE: *(Continuing; gasping after her)* That's it — leave us.

NORA: *(Walking and cursing)* "...hour of our death, Amen," he's mad and he's driven her mad, and he's trying to drive me mad —

JOYCE: Where are you sneaking away to, now?

NORA: *(Stopping)* I am walking to Mass.

JOYCE: Crawling, you mean.

NORA: Rave on, but it's her religion she needs now.

JOYCE: Who?

NORA: Our daughter, who d'ye think?

JOYCE: Which religion? There're a hundred and forty-two known religions. And what good would it do her?

NORA: Give her a bit of hope, which is more than you've done. And help her to face the next life.

JOYCE: WHAT ABOUT THIS LIFE?! — And how could I give her any hope when I've none myself?

NORA: You've never known your own daughter.

JOYCE: Allow me to say, I was present at her conception.

NORA: You know nothin' at all about women.

JOYCE: I know all that can be known.

NORA: And I know the rest! — Sure, you've not a clue about your own self, so how could you understand anything about Lucia?

JOYCE: Lucia does not need "understanding" — Lucia needs love!

NORA: Words! I'm — away — now — to —

JOYCE: Mass, I know. Dominick go frisk him! My God, the woman still believes in banshees and the Holy Ghost!

NORA: Shut yer gob.

JOYCE: To pray for her?

(First NORA, then JOYCE, break down.)

NORA: To pray for all of us.

(JOYCE collapses in her arms.)

JOYCE: The book, the book, I traded my daughter's youth for that book!

NORA: *(She rocks him like a child.)* Wisha, Jim, hush, hush....

JOYCE: Never a real home — no country, no language, no friends —

NORA: We've made our bed, Jim....

JOYCE: The drink! — I traded her soul to the devil. The virginity of her soul! — For the book! The critics were right — I'm not a writer at all, I'm a devil!

NORA: Yes, you're a "Great Sinner" — except you're not — you're just an ordinary one. *(A bitter laugh)*

JOYCE: You're a cruel woman! Trot away now to Mass, and chat up the priest.

NORA: You're pathetic. *(She starts to leave.)*

JOYCE: "Pray in your closet."

NORA: Raving.

JOYCE: The Bible says — "Pray in your — "

NORA: You pray in your closet!

JOYCE: I would if I had one.

NORA: A closet?

JOYCE: No. A soul.

NORA: You poor fellah, you — no one has a soul, until they've confessed their sins, and Communion taken.

JOYCE: What? What is there left for me to confess?

NORA: *(Coming back to him, she speaks softly to his heart or soul.)* Yourself.

JOYCE: Myself?

NORA: I'm not talkin' about the guilt — the drink and the writing and the guilt. I'm referrin' to Jimmy Joyce — the man.

(He shakes, then kneels in front of her like a child.)

NORA: *(Continuing)* Jim, get up now!

JOYCE: I confess.

NORA: Have you no shame, at all?

(His tone stuns her. He is not mocking.)

JOYCE: No! — I confess.... You hear my confession. You give me my forgiveness. Not a priest — you!

NORA: Jim, what are you doing? — I can't forgive you. I can't give —

JOYCE: Only you —

NORA: — can't give you Communion. I'm only —

JOYCE: I'll take anything! *(A sobbing laugh; he clings to her dress.)*

NORA: Let me go, now —

JOYCE: No! I confess!

NORA: Then go and do it!

(She rips away from him. He falls over on all fours, crawls a few feet, then, like a beast in pain, he tries to pray. He makes only strange sounds.)

NORA: *(Continuing)* Christ have pity on the poor thing....

JOYCE: *(His voice is strangled.)* Christ have mercy....

(NORA sways with the shared pain. She fights to keep her voice private and under control. His words are like a death rattle.)

NORA: "Holy Mary, pray for him...."

JOYCE: "All you holy Angels and Archangels, pray for...."

NORA: "St. Joseph..." Oh, please, don't let him die, now....

JOYCE: "St. Mary Magdalene..."

NORA: — let him die in Zurich — where we began....

JOYCE: "Through your death and burial... Run out to meet her, Angels of the Lord...."

(He vomits dryly, in spasms of grief.)

NORA: — let them both die there....

(Slowly, like an animal, his panting subsides. Then, he looks up with exhausted cunning.)

JOYCE: Will you give me the Communion, now?

(NORA is wary. She brings a towel to wipe his face. He looks up at her.)

NORA: What is it you're after, now?... What d'ye want from me, Jim?

JOYCE: Everything: Open my tomb — speak in tongues — fill me with the Holy Ghost — erection and resurrection — ravish my soul — put your wafer in my mouth....

(NORA stares down at the mad outburst with a cold control.)

NORA: What else?

JOYCE: Sing a dirty song for me.

NORA: *(Pause, a whisper)* Oh, you're as cute as a shit-house rat! — You want me to beat you — but I won't.

(He laughs silently, shaking his head, then lets her help him up. She has to guide him to the sofa.)

NORA: No... No, I'm a dead man. Dead and rotten...

NORA: Wisha, Jim, give over. — You're not a great sinner, you're a great writer, that's all, the greatest writer in the world. It's not your fault. It's no one's fault, and that's the short of it.

JOYCE: Just let me die — and sell the manuscripts.

NORA: Sure, you're worth more dead that alive. *(A sad laugh)* We all are. That's the truth: We're all dying. — But I wouldn't give the critics the satisfaction.

(Sound of church bells)

JOYCE: That was the dream —

NORA: Lie down.

JOYCE: — that I had last night...

NORA: Shh.

JOYCE: Terrible dream...

NORA: Lie down, you're worn out completely.

JOYCE: I was crossing the Liffey — over O'Connell Bridge — and there was a man on each side of me....

NORA: I'll put a quilt on you.

JOYCE: The bells for the dead were tolling....

NORA: There — stretch out.

JOYCE: St. Michans' bells tolling.... And the two men...

NORA: I tell you what —

JOYCE: —they each took me by the elbows — to cross over....

(A long pause. NORA moves, at last, but her leg is worse, so she tries to limber it as she prepares to leave.)

NORA: Ah! Jesus, Mary, and Joseph — ah, the devil — Mother Mary. *(Walking; laughs)* What did Kathleen's lad say: "Matthew, Mark, look at John!" — ha, put that in your book. Mmm, sure it'll limber up if I walk out to the post —

JOYCE: Bring me the galleys, will you?

(NORA sets JOYCE up at his writing table to correct the already printed copy of Finnegan's Wake, *for a future edition.)*

NORA: *(Referring to manuscript)* Here's your chop suey.

JOYCE: Irish stew.

NORA: Word salad.

JOYCE: *(With a flourish)* "Schizophrenia." *(Quoting from* Hamlet*)* "A document in madness."

(He freezes. The words stand for their daughter, Lucia, who suffers from the dread disease.)

NORA: Nay, nay, Jim. You must stop now. Give up the guilt, once and for all, or come out with me to Mass.

JOYCE: *(In clenched pain)* Dominick go frisk him.

NORA: Aye, you're a scandalous man. But you didn't "create" Lucia, or her madness, like you did this, she's not a character in a book.

JOYCE: Deus absconditus.

NORA: Speak English, or Eyetalian, or French if you want me to understand.

JOYCE: God's run away.

NORA: Run away? *(Laughs)* Since when did you believe in God — on His throne on high, or runnin' away like a gombeen-man without paying the hotel bill?

JOYCE: *(A deep bitterness)* Hail Mary, Full of grease, The Lard is with thee!

NORA: Don't take His name in vain.

JOYCE: Who, God? — He doesn't exist — the bastard!

(They laugh, then pause, sadly.)

NORA: Well, it's like this.... It's like the Liffey....

(Picks up the manuscript)

NORA: The men came in your dream to escort you right across.

JOYCE: Mmm...

NORA: Across to the other side. — But you wouldn't have none of it — not from God nor Death nor nobody, so you jumped into the river and dived to the bottom and hid down there in the caves and corners.

JOYCE: Are you writing my dreams, now?

NORA: ...But Lucia...she didn't dive in....

JOYCE: No... She fell.

NORA: Aye. — To the bottom...

JOYCE: *(Softly)* "Good-night, Ladies."

(Pause. NORA sits him down.)

NORA: Do a little work. Torture the paper. Add a couple a' commas. Sure, it's the great book, altogether superior to the other.... If there's no word at the post, I'll go look for Giorgio and Stephen. — I've put something on the ring to warm.

JOYCE: I couldn't eat a morsel.

NORA: We'll see about that. — Now, I'm going to cable Miss Weaver, and the sanitarium, that we intend to talk to the doctors and the staff about Lucia's future — talk to 'em in person. And then I'll be back. Here's your tea.... All right? — And you can rest easy that all bills of Lucia's will be paid.... The money'll be here. — How do I know? It's that simple: Harriet Weaver is a woman of independent wealth who believes it's a sin not to share it with a man of genius. Is that true or not?

JOYCE: More or less.

NORA: While in you, on the other hand, we have a man who believes that the world owes him a livin'. The two of yez was made for each other. *(Laughs)* A match made in heaven to the tune of half-a-million pounds, glory be to God.

JOYCE: Matthew, Mark, look at Jim.

(She pauses to trigger a favorite ritual: mockery of "The Writer." They use exaggerated accents, again.)

NORA: It's a queer kind of work, writin' — very queer. Always has been.

JOYCE: Ach, but sure, doesn't it pay the big money?

NORA: Begod, it does that.

JOYCE: Bejabus — and be the hour, too.

NORA: And all the swank "artistes" that's put their families in their ink pots, and run away to Paris... *(As herself:)* ...to dine out on their lives.

(The joke is over. JOYCE *speaks normally.)*

JOYCE: ...Proust.

NORA: Very queer, Marcel Proust.

JOYCE: Why?

NORA: A very peculiar class a' man.

JOYCE: Not at all.

NORA: Well...the two of you talking about his parrot, and where to get the best meal for the money.

JOYCE: ...Paris.

NORA: Hmm... It's all a dream now.... Well, don't stand there like the ghost of a — *(Laughs)* ...You have to go back to work, man, we have to live.

*(*JOYCE*, to keep her from leaving, tries to provoke another "game." She lets herself be drawn in for a moment, before leaving.)*

JOYCE: I am working. *(Laughs)* Oh, aye, I know —

NORA: "A writer is always working," haven't I heard that three hundred and sixty-five days a year. — All right, I'm leavin'. You work.

JOYCE: I am. I'm thinking.

NORA: Prove it.

JOYCE: If I don't get a large whiskey my mind will give way.

NORA: A "large whiskey"? But yer Lordship always taught me there was no such thing. — Whenever your Lowness took a "drop of the creature", after a long night's work.

JOYCE: Sure, didn't I march with Father Murphey and General Humbert and Dauntless Kelly in the rising of '98?

NORA: *(Laughs)* Go to work, you lazy grafter.

JOYCE: *(Hidden laughter)* The shop's closed; the Boycott, you know.

(Their exchange has the casual virtuosity of two masters whose minds are as one: sheer grace, effortless and perfect.)

NORA: What shop would that be, yer Honor?

JOYCE: "Barnacle — Joyce and Co." In the town of Anus Mundi.

(Their voices could be out of the Dublin depths, again:)

NORA: Oh, you mean the "pun factory"?

JOYCE: Hmm — the "orifice" is closed till the midnight hour.

NORA: For the duration of the "troubles"?

JOYCE: Amen.

NORA: Who told you such a terrible tale?

JOYCE: The local rabblement.

NORA: Ahh... What became of the old man, then, who used to run it, did they say?

JOYCE: Ahh, that he was, ah, crucified on the cross of his "cruelfiction".

NORA: But is it the "Gospel" truth?

JOYCE: It's the holy smoke.

NORA: Suffering Jaysus, and whatever became of his family, at all — did they tell ye that?

JOYCE: Nothin'. They sank — without a trace — into Dublin Bay....

NORA: Well... It was "Finn" while it lasted....

(The exercise is over for the day; the great players bow invisibly to each other.)

NORA: *(Continuing)* ...All right, then, I'll be back.... Now, "sup all and say naught."

(She exits.)

(Act break may be taken here.)

(NORA exits. JOYCE tries to "work," using a magnifying glass. He holds up the manuscript to his eye, makes a correction — laughs and curses to himself. Exhausted, he takes off his glasses, dips his napkin in the tea, bathes his eyes. Leans back, his eyes unprotected and gazing.)

(In a fugue of grief for his daughter, JOYCE begins by calling up, from Hamlet, *the mad Ophelia.)*

JOYCE: *(Softly to himself)* "A document in madness, thoughts and remembrances mixed... There's rue for you and here's some for me.... *(Sings)* "And will he not come again...? Good night, sweet Ladies." *(Looking up, whispering)* Can't someone help my wonder-wild child — Lucia?... Jung-Freud... When she was Jung and easily Freudened....

(He smiles and the pain is eased as his mind wanders. But, unable to see to write fluently, he must create out loud. He begins with a snatch of song from Twelfth Night, *with great sweetness:* "O Mistress Mine.")

JOYCE: *(Continuing)* "What is love, is not hereafter.... Then come kiss me sweet and twenty; Youth's a stuff will not endure."

(He smiles, dreaming.... Then picks up the manuscript to his eye, then down.)

JOYCE: *(Continuing, laughs)* "Looney in my loneness." *(Puts manuscript down)* "For all their faults. I am passing out. O bitter ending." *(Chuckles, drinks tea)* "I'll slip away before they're up. They'll never see. Nor know. Nor miss me. And it's old and old it's sad and old it's sad and weary I go back to you, my cold father, my cold mad father.... Whish! A gull. Gulls. Far calls. Coming, far! End here. Us then. Finn, again! Take... *(Standing)* ...mememormee! till thousandsthee. Lips. The keys to. Given! A way a lone a last a loved a long the"...

(He has made a definitive statement through the stream of the words; he feels purged, more free. So, he goes to the gramophone and clumsily starts up the John McCormack record, again, this time singing along in good voice to "The Star of the County Down". Lights fade, indicating a short passage of time, if no act break has been taken.)

JOYCE: *(Continuing)* "Near Banbridge Town
in the County Down
one morning last July,
From a boreen green
came a sweet Colleen
and she smiled as she passed me by.

She looked so sweet
from her two bare feet
to the sheen of her nut-brown hair,
Such a coaxin' elf
Sure I shook myself
for to see I was really there."

(NORA enters. He sings to her in performance style, then starts to jig and dance, till winded.)

NORA: All right, well, there's life in ye yet. *(Laughs)* Lepping and streeling, jigging and reeling. Faith, you look like a —

JOYCE: Death on wires!

NORA: Ah, well, there's some sap in ye yet.

JOYCE: *(They laugh.)* He's not still alive, is he?

NORA: How do you feel, now?

JOYCE: "And on the third day He rose."

NORA: Don't start that, again, now.

(She turns off the music.)

JOYCE: Did you walk the streets or go to Mass?

NORA: I did. I went to Mass.

JOYCE: Is He still dead?

(Laughing behind his hand)

NORA: Don't try to be clever.

(NORA takes a packet of visas out of her prayer book. JOYCE shrinks in fear.)

JOYCE: *(Whispers; peers through his magnifying glass)* What is it?

NORA: The visas for Zurich. — They won't bite you.

JOYCE: I'm too ill. What's to become of Lucia?

NORA: *(She starts to pack up the cases.)* No hurry, no rush. *(She hums to reassure him.)*

JOYCE: Ah, well, that's all right, then.... Did the money arrive?

NORA: What?

JOYCE: Did the money arrive?

NORA: *(Still packing)* No.

JOYCE: Sell everything!

NORA: You're feverish.

JOYCE: No, I'm completely restored. I feel so strong I'm going to take a brisk walk —

NORA: Oh, no —

JOYCE: To the lavatory.

(He goes into the bedroom. Sings, off. Alone, NORA rubs her leg for relief. Then, she goes to the telephone and talks very quietly.)

NORA: Hallo... This is Madame Joyce — Oui, Monsieur Giorgio Joyce at... um, est-ce que Monsieur Giorgio Joyce se trouve au bar? *(She listens, sighs.)* ...Merci, ah, if he comes in.... Oui, oui, merci, c'est tres important.

(She hangs up and resumes packing, as JOYCE re-enters.)

JOYCE: Inform the Holy See! I'm completely cured. Miracleous phenomenonous: the old verbal convolvulis is abated; the adjectival spasms? Vanished! The logorrhea and the syncopated shite — complete remission! *(His energy is used up. He smiles, like a boy, at* NORA. *Softly:)* The old song and dance...

(She nods. He stares out again. NORA *watches him. Then* NORA *takes out a letter. The two stand rooted, gazing at each other in a shared spasm of pain.)*

JOYCE: ...Lucia?

NORA: It is.

JOYCE: Read it.

NORA: I will.... *(Reading with desperate control)* "Father dear, I am very fond of you. Thanks for the pretty pen. Zurich is not the worst place in the world, is it? Maybe one day you can come with me to the museum, Father. I think that you are spending a lot of money on me. Father, if you want to go back to Paris, you would do well to do so. Father dear, I have had too nice a life. I am spoiled. You must both forgive me. I hope that you will come here again. Father, if ever I take a fancy to anybody, I swear to you on the head of Jesus that it will not be because I am not fond of you. Do not forget that. I don't really know what I am writing, Father. At Prangins I saw a number of artists, especially women who seemed to me all very hysterical. Am I to turn out like them? No, it would be better to sell shoes if that can be done with simplicity and truth. And besides, I don't know whether all this I am writing means anything to you.

"I should like to have a life as quiet as I have now, with a garden and perhaps a dog, but nobody is ever contented, isn't that so? So many people were envious of me and of Mama because you are too good. It is a pity that you don't like Ireland, for after all, it is a lovely country, if I may judge by the pictures I have seen, and the stories I have heard. Who knows what fate has in store for us? At any rate, in spite of the fact that life seems full of light this evening, here, if ever I should go away, it would be to a country which belongs in a way to you, isn't that true, Father? I am still writing silly things, you see.

"I send you both affectionate greetings, and I hope that you did not miss your train the other day. —Lucia"

(They stand staring for a very long moment in unspeakable anguish, then pick up the threads of their life again.)

JOYCE: *(Continuing)* Will we have a Christmas feast this year?

NORA: What? — Can you take some food now?

JOYCE: What? Oh, I don't know. Something very light.

NORA: Eggs? *(She cleans up his writing table.)*

JOYCE: Jesus, no.

NORA: Well, make up your mind, or leave it to me.

JOYCE: *(He kicks at an open trunk.)* Leave it be, for pity's sake, it's all rubbish, we'll sort it out next week.... Yes, we'll have a Christmas party — for the boy.

NORA: *(More packing)* We'll have it in Zurich, then.

JOYCE: Wherever we have it. — And champagne.

NORA: For "the boy"? — There, now.

(JOYCE is wearing down again. NORA tries to keep his mood up.)

NORA: *(Continuing)* Sure, we'll lay something on, no matter where. The boy's mad for his sweets.

JOYCE: Your mother was a born cook.

NORA: Sure, we all are. We learned how over an open turf fire back in the Stone Age.

(She returns to her cooking.)

JOYCE: ...What would he fancy, the boy?

NORA: You tell me.

JOYCE: Ah, well, there's your rhubarb pudding with the meringue topping....

NORA: Oh, aye, and the baked apples wrapped in pastry.

(JOYCE is enjoying a pang of hunger. He drifts over to observe NORA's culinary efforts.)

JOYCE: Mm... Pudding cake...

NORA: Mm... Stand there.

JOYCE: What's that?

NORA: Syrup of figs.

JOYCE: Who's it for?

NORA: You.

JOYCE: No.

NORA: It is. It'll wash you out.

JOYCE: Well... Damson jam, do you think? For the Christmas breakfast.

NORA: Now, where would I —

JOYCE: And barm bracks.

NORA: Barm bracks?

JOYCE: Definately.

NORA: Is it Hallowe'en you're talking about or Christmas?

JOYCE: Definately. With a ring inside for Stephen.

NORA: For the boy.

JOYCE: Yes.

NORA: *(Laughs)* When you put one on as a wedding ring — I could've killed you — blatherin' that you only wore it because it "eased" your hand from "the writer's cramp."

JOYCE: *(Dreaming and drifting)* ...Rice pudding and tarts... and treacle bread...

NORA: Stand over there, will ye?

JOYCE: What's that?

NORA: Fillet of salmon.

JOYCE: Mm.

NORA: Very mild...

JOYCE: The boy's mad for "boxty".

NORA: Mm.

JOYCE: Your mother made it the best.
"Boxty on the griddle, boxty in the pan
If you don't eat boxty you'll never get a man."

NORA: She had a "secret Galwegian recipe."

JOYCE: What?

NORA: Sit down till I'm through. — Mm? Oh, umm, let's see. She'd take the raw potatoes; grate 'em in muslin cloth; mix 'em with flour; salt 'em; shape 'em into dumplings — move aside will ye, Jim? — boil 'em —

JOYCE: The dumplings?

NORA: Sweet Grace above — the dumplings. Boil 'em in a big pot till they were lovely grey and slimy; then slice 'em thin and fry 'em with eggs....

JOYCE: Then eat 'em.

NORA: *(A burst of laughter)* Yes! — Here, dry your lips, sure, you're droolin'.

JOYCE: Annie Barnacle's "secret recipe".

NORA: Mm.

JOYCE: *(Pause)* "Her portrait has passed."

(NORA, *too, remembers the phrase from* The Portrait of the Artist.)

JOYCE: *(Continuing, pause)* What else?

NORA: What else what?

JOYCE: What else did we used to eat? — Sherry trifle? Pickled pigs trotters?

NORA: Is it your memory that's goin', now? Let me alone and they'll be back within the hour and you'll have your dinner. For a thin man, you're a terrible glutton.

JOYCE: My mother, now, put currants in her barm bracks —

NORA: No, now, let's talk about Zurich and Christmas and not Ireland and the *(Sings)* "dear dead days beyond recall," forty years and more ago. Please.

JOYCE: *(Sings a pure phrase)* "Just a song at twilight..."

NORA: *(Pause)* They'll be back any time, now.

JOYCE: If he's taken the boy into the hotel bar, I'll cut him out of my will as I would and "embossed carbuncle"!

NORA: *(Laughs)* Your will? Is it King Lear you are, now —

JOYCE: My son is a drunkard. When he has the money. Full stop. Don't argue with me. You're as blind when it comes to him as I am when I try to see the proofs of my —

NORA: As you are — when it comes to Lucia!

JOYCE: That's enough, then.

NORA: She had a glee eye as a child, but, no, you told people that she "looked like Norma Shearer"!

JOYCE: *(Pause)* I intend to dine in the hotel restaurant today, for my stomach's sake.

NORA: Will you listen — the man will say anything at all.

JOYCE: I want a piece of red meat, I tell you — I'm that bored.

NORA: You think that you're "bored"?!

(She resumes packing.)

JOYCE: *(Pause)* You've sex on your mind — night and day.

NORA: In the mind, not on it, in it. Sex in the mind and in the book — not the bed, the book. A book so dirty that in America it drove them into the streets to fornicate. Ahh, but that's "Literature".

(Slamming cases)

JOYCE: Philistine.

NORA: Irishman!

JOYCE: Prude.

NORA: Panderer.

JOYCE: Peasant. Puritan.

NORA: Pervert.

JOYCE: Censor.

NORA: Pornographer.

JOYCE: Critic!

NORA: No one can call me that! *(She throws a utensil.)* You drunken sleeveen.

JOYCE: I've a drink taken —

NORA: — Hah! A bucketful.

JOYCE: — A sup taken in my time —

NORA: — Ha-ha! You've drunk the Liffey in your time!

JOYCE: — But I-am-not-a-drunk!

NORA: You'll do till the genuine article comes along!

JOYCE: I'm going down to the bar to see if they're —

NORA: Oh, no, you're not! The only place you're goin' is Zurich!

(NORA blocks his way. JOYCE puts on his hat and tries to take off his dressing gown but NORA wrestles him to a stand still. Both shout at each other at the same time, wearing their voices down to a croaking melody. NORA's pace is staccato, with no pause, while JOYCE speaks in short bursts, breathing hard.)

NORA:
I'll murder ye, ye cursagod, you. Ye little shoneen, you. Ye big boozer, you. You ignorant gombeen, you — Raise your hand to me, will you, you dirty jackeen, you yahoo, you. Satan *(Pronounced satin)*, get ye behind me. With your Paddy whiskey and your cork in and your Dutch urage — Its' a matter for police — I'll have your ndson baptized, and have christened — I'm goin' e priest now — not a writer at all, d everybody — used n family —

JOYCE:
How dare you? Get away and get out. I take the odd drop as a "medicament" and you pounce on me like the bag of cats that you are. — Let go! I'll have a glass of porter before the midday meal, if I fancy it.
(Coughing)
It's because I'm in pain! You've no mercy. You're a peasant and you've no idea the comfort in a ball of hot malt when you're in pain.
(He pants, recovers, resumes.)
I'll have a small Irish and Apollinairis! *(With a flourish, as Falstaff)*

put 'em in your dirty
book —
used me, inside and out,
early and late...
...girl and woman — used me,
with no shame and no
thanks! — It's a matter
for the police now, I'm
going to have you LOCKED UP
with Lucia —

"Bring me a bottle of sack
and put a cheeze in't!"
I'll go out on the road, I
tell you, like Tolstoy —
I'll walk across Europe
with my child, my daughter —
like Tolstoy, like Lear!

(They have run down. He collapses in her arms. They have heard and hurt each other. He quotes Lear; her head falls on his chest. She sighs, "Jim, ah, Jim.")

JOYCE: "No, no, no, no: Come let's away to prison,
We two alone will sing like birds i'th'cage:
...So we'll live and pray and sing, and tell old tales,
and laugh at gilded butterflies...who loses and who wins;
who's in, who's out; and take upon's the mystery of things
as if we were God's spies...."

(They embrace a long moment. NORA leads him to the sofa, again. Both are staggering.)

NORA: Jim, to please me will you think about the future and what's to come, and forget about what's past, and can't be helped or changed.

JOYCE: The "future" — my son in a bar, my daughter in a...and it's my doing. The sins of the father....

(She lies next to him to rest.)

NORA: Nay, nay, if there's a mill-race in the blood that pumps out the future of the children — if there's such a thing as "genes" at all, then our children or the next man's — Kelly or Coy or Concannon — sure, all the children are born out of Ireland!

JOYCE: What's that?

NORA: Like you wrote in the new book, in *Finnegans Wake* —

JOYCE: You haven't read it!

NORA: Never mind — I know what's in it.

JOYCE: What?

NORA: "Here comes everybody"!

(JOYCE laughs a long sigh of delight.)

JOYCE: Here comes everybody.... Is that what you're trying to tell me about the children?

NORA: Now do you see?

JOYCE: So that I won't succumb to the old schuld, the old "agenbite inwit," the old guilt, the old Adam, the old —

NORA: Yes!

JOYCE: *(Pause)* Yes... It's Ireland. At the end of the day, one way or another, that's what it is.

NORA: Ireland.

JOYCE: I'm her worst enemy.

NORA: Not while I'm alive.

(Their mutual curse has a lyric quality, so that the tone of voice somewhat contradicts the cruel words.)

JOYCE: She drives her artists mad, then they drive their children mad.

NORA: It's an asylum.

JOYCE: "...This lovely land that always sent
Her writers into banishment
And in a spirit of Irish fun
Betrayed her own leaders, one by one
'Twas Irish humor, wet and dry,
Flung quicklime into Parnell's eye...."

NORA: Granny Simmons said, "Sure, St. Patrick was a gentleman, he came from "dacent" people."

(Her savage caricature makes them both laugh grimly.)

JOYCE: Ah, well, it's a dung heap.

NORA: A graveyard.

JOYCE: An old sow that eats her own farrow.

NORA: Narrow as a pig's back.

JOYCE: The dullness, the ignorance, the bigotry, the —

NORA: The climate.

JOYCE: The women in church, the men in pubs.

NORA: The "Men"! Sure, the men are dead or gone to America, leavin' the women in their thousands to run wild, turned sour and single, a race of old maids and sex maniacs, it's enough to make you savage!

JOYCE: Didn't the critic for the *Catholic World* completely discourage Giorgio about his singing voice and turn him into an alcoholic?

NORA: It's mad Ireland that hurt you into poetry, and that's the alls of it, and thank you very much. To hell with 'em, entirely... Now, that's enough, now. That's *(Singing)* "the dear dead days beyond recall." — Keep your thoughts on Zurich, now, can't ye?

JOYCE: *(Pause; sighing)* Where will it end, Nora?

NORA: Zurich. It was good enough for us in 1915, it's good enough for us now. Ah, sure, what's the difference, you're world-famous, now.... You'll find your health there, again. You were always very partial to the "cuisine" in Zurich.

(Again, with great skill she has steered him back toward life. She completes the packing.)

JOYCE: That's true. Didn't I write home about it?... "Ten-thirty a.m. Ham, bread and butter, and coffee; one-thirty p.m. Soup, roast lamb, and..." *(Sinking down)* But that was a World War ago....

NORA: Listen here to me, now: It was roast lamb and potatoes and bread and wine; four p.m. was beef stew, bread, and wine — you remember the wine?

JOYCE: Wonderful! — Six p.m. Roast veal, bread, cheese and wine; eight-thirty p.m. Roast veal, bread and grapes, and vermouth — hmm...

NORA: Nine-thirty p.m. Veal cutlets, bread, salad, grapes, and wine.

JOYCE: And we still went to bed hungry.

NORA: We did, we did!

JOYCE: And then you'd make a man of me.

NORA: Mmm...

JOYCE: *(Laughs softly)* But not enough of one... It's too clean — Zurich — too bloody clean....

(He smiles, closing his eyes. NORA tries to rise quietly. JOYCE reaches up to hold her hand. He hums a phrase and she takes it up, to sing him to sleep.)

NORA: "...and the flickering shadows softly come and go,
Though the heart be weary..." *(She sings and he seems to drift off, but still holding onto her.)* "...love's old sweet song."

(NORA stands still, holding on to his hand. He mumbles something too low for her to catch. She talks to him, now, in a completely maternal tone.)

NORA: *(Continuing)* Not a word out of you, now... Hmm, clingin' like a barnacle.

JOYCE: ...the Irish, they'll curse you....

NORA: Wisha...

JOYCE: ...in two languages...

NORA: Wisha...the Lord Mayor of Dublin sent out for a pound of chops for his dinner....

JOYCE: ...Dublin...

NORA: Wisha, a pound of chops...what kind of people is going at all, now?

(JOYCE *turns in pain, almost asleep, still muttering.* NORA *calms him with her voice.*)

JOYCE: ...Mememormee...

NORA: Sure, I remember you, I remember you....

(JOYCE's *dream talk is understood only by* NORA. *Their voices sing to each other; the sense is in the sound. Overlapping:*)

JOYCE: Ivernia...Caitlin Ni Houlihan...Anna Livia...

NORA: Wisha, shh, I know — it's Ireland you've been dreamin' of for forty years, shh....

JOYCE: Shan Van Vocht...the poor owl' woman...

NORA: Shhh, aye, and the three queens of Eire, and the old woman, and me dark Rosaleen... Shhh...

JOYCE: Mememormee...

NORA: Shhh, give over, Jim, listen to me, now: You'll be right as rain back in Zurich. Walkin' with Giorgio — you'll be a new man and so will he. You won't touch a drop, and you'll both be yourselves again — for the boy's sake, for peace's sake. You'll land on your feet, there. You'll take the air, and I'll cook for yez. All your favorites — tripe and onions with white sauce; roast chicken stuffed with mashed potatoes, hmmm...

(JOYCE *breathes regularly, now, still clutching her hand. There is an occasional word or sound from him.*)

NORA: *(Continuing)* Shh... Sure, it's I'll help with your proofs, again. And Miss Weaver, she'll get the royalty money through to us, somehow, no need to worry... Shh — and I'll cook hot grocers' peas for yez, and even corned beef, and colcannon with butter and onions and kale and turnips like Annie Barnacle did, and boiled eggs and rashers with slices of tomatoes — the way you used to wolf it down.... *(She sings again.)* "Though the way be weary..." — Soft days, and then we'll have Lucia with us again; sure, this war'll be over in no time, and we'll have her back — sure, God shuts one door and opens another.... *(Resisting her own grief) (Continuing)* Shh... And chops of lamb and pork... We'll have her back, like she was, before.... And for your birthday, leg of lamb with fresh peas and parsnips and... *(She breaks for a moment.)* ...turnips... Christmas breakfast — bacon and eggs and blood sausage — and then a goose at four o'clock and a Limerick ham... And we'll all sing the old songs around the piano, and we'll dance, too — you'll see. And they'll come from all over the world to call on us. All the little fellahs like Hemingway and Gide and Proust — no, he's dead —

(JOYCE *mumbles something in his sleep about* Rahoon.)

NORA: *(Continuing)* "Rahoon" is it? Sure, I know it by heart:
"Rain on Rahoon falls softly, softly falling,
Where my dark lover lies.
Sad is his voice that calls me, sadly calling
At grey moonrise...."
Sure, aren't they all buried there? Annie Barnacle and me poor dumb Da, too, and Michael Bodkin, that poor boy that loved me and that you've been jealous of, for nothin', all these years — because you were my first and only one, Jim, and that's the Gospel alls of it.... *(NORA waits a moment until he seems to drop off. A warning siren in the distance.* NORA *goes to the telephone and whispers into it.)* S'il-vous-plait, le porter pour les...oui, send the man up for the luggage, tout de suite — comprenez-vous? — oui, merci, tout de suite....

(She tip-toes back to the couch. Church bells sound. JOYCE *seems to have stopped breathing.* NORA, *in fear, shakes his hand until he stirs.)*

JOYCE: What?

NORA: Open your eyes, now, Jim. You gave me a turn. Or were you only play actin', as usual? Get up, now, it's late in the day. *(She tries to move.)* Aii, I'm frozen with the arthi-ritis, standin' here. Get up, now. You have to eat!

JOYCE: I can't.

NORA: No back-chat, now. Up. *(Laughs)* "The conscience of his race," and the man's so lazy he won't move a muscle. Layin' there like a boy. *(She touches him.)* Is he still dead?

JOYCE: What?

NORA: Ahh, has he, ah, risen?

JOYCE: Ahh — no.

NORA: Ahh, well — no matter... Stand up, now, before they get here.

JOYCE: "Love, hear thou
How soft, how sad his voice is ever calling,
Ever unanswered and the dark rain falling,
Then as now." *(He sits up.)* Tell me the truth, Nora, at last. Was he your first love?

(She looks down, smiles, strokes his hair.)

NORA: Ah, Jim, Jim, simple-minded Jim... You're still a boy. Still the Dublin boy with the frown and the eyes of an angel; in your overcoat that hung down to your feet; your shoes with the heels worn off, and that big white sombrero. *(Laughs)* You're still a boy.

JOYCE: He loved you.

NORA: He died for me.

JOYCE: I lived for you. And now I'm old.

NORA: Still a boy.

(The warning sirens sound again, nearer. A knock at the door, and NORA *begins to sing "Off to Philadelphia in the Morning". Slowly,* JOYCE *joins her. She pushes a trunk.)*

NORA: *(Continuing)* Yes — we're ready. — "O, my name is Paddy Daley from a spot called Tipperary —"

JOYCE & NORA:
"I lately took the notion for to cross the briny ocean
And I start for Philadelphia in the mornin' —"

(He is up. They begin to dance, slowly and sickly, then with growing energy. Sunlight from the window captures them, shadows lengthen, music rises; and another loud knock....)

JOYCE & NORA: *(Continuing)*
"Oh, my name is Paddy Daley from a spot called Tipperary —"

(They jig and sing, laughing and loving, forever young as the lights go down. Two months later, JAMES JOYCE *was dead.)*

THE END

THE STAR OF THE COUNTY DOWN

Near Banbridge Town
in the County Down
one morning last July,
From a boreen green
came a sweet Colleen
and she smiled as she passed me by.

She looked so sweet
from her two bare feet
to the sheen of her nut-brown hair,
Such a coaxin' elf
Sure I shook myself
for to see I was really there.

Chorus: From Bantry Bay
up to Derry Quay
and from Galway to Dublin Town,
no maid I've seen
like the grand colleen
that I met in the County Down.

As she onward sped
sure I scratched my head,
and I looked with a feelin' rare,
And I says, says I
to a passer-by
"Who's the maid with the nut-brown hair?"
He smiled at me
and he says, says he,
That's the gem in Ireland's Crown,
Young Rosy McCann
from the banks of the Bann,
she's the star of the County Down.

Chorus: From Bantry Bay
up to Derry Quay
and from Galway to Dublin Town,
no maid I've seen

like the grand colleen
that I met in the County Down.

At the harvest fair
she'll be surely there
and I'll dress in my Sunday clothes,
With me shoes shone bright
and me hat cocked right
for a smile from my nut-brown Rose.

No pipe I'll smoke,
no horse I'll yoke,
'till me plough is a rust-colored brown,
'till a smiling bride
by my own fireside,
Sits the star of the County Down.

OFF TO PHILADELPHIA

Oh me name is Paddy Daley,
from a spot called Tipperary,
the heart of all the girls I'm a thorn in....
But before the break of morn
faith 'tis they'll be all forlorn,
for I'm off the Philadelphia in the mornin'.

Chorus: With me bundle on me shoulder,
faith there's no man could be bolder,
for I'm leavin' dear Ireland without warnin'.
For I lately took the notion,
for to cross the briny ocean,
and I start for Philadelphia in the mornin'.

There's a girl called Kate Malone
whom I'd hoped to call my own,
and to see my little cabin floor adornin'.
But my heart is sad and weary,
how can she be Missus Leary,
as I start for Philadelphia in the mornin'.

Chorus: When they told me I must leave this place,
I tried to keep a cheerful face
For sure me heart beats sorrow, I was scornin'.
But the tears will surely blind me
for the friends I leave behind me
when I start for Philadelphia in the mornin'.

Chorus: Though me bundle's on me shoulder,
and there's no man could be bolder,
though I'd leave to see the spot that I was born in,
yet someday I'll take the notion,
to come back across the ocean
to my home in dear old Ireland, in the mornin'.